The Pacific Forum Line

The Pacific Forum Line

A commitment to regional shipping

Tony Nightingale

Clerestory Press
1998

ISBN 0–9583706–5–6

Published with the assistance of the Pacific Forum Line.

Cover photographs:
Front cover: The *Forum Samoa* at Pago Pago, American Samoa.
Back cover: The *Forum New Zealand II* at Brisbane.
            The flags of the shareholder nations.

Published by Clerestory Press
P.O. Box 21-120, Christchurch, New Zealand

Typesetting by TypeShop, Christchurch
Printed by The Caxton Press, Christchurch.

Foreword

By Ratu Sir Kamisese Mara
GCMG, KBE, KtStJ, President of Fiji

THE FORUM SHIPPING LINE was one of the dreams articulated by Pacific Island leaders at the first South Pacific Conference I ever attended, at Nasinu in 1956, where His Majesty the King of Tonga—then entitled Tupouto'a and Prime Minister—was chairman of the Economic Committee. With typical far-sightedness, he underlined the need for sea transport amongst the islands as the artery for our economic development.

The present King, first as Prime Minister and when he ascended the throne, showed us the way. The Kingdom of Tonga not only had ships built overseas but even experimented with rubberised containers in the shape of giant sausages, filled with fuel and towed between Fiji and Tonga.

President Hammer DeRoburt launched larger ships to carry the much-needed water and other necessities for his country's requirements. The British Phosphate Commission had ships to transport its product from Nauru to New Zealand before Nauru acquired the phosphate industry.

The Kiribati government, from colonial days to the present, has provided ships for transportation between Kiribati and Fiji. The British Solomon Islands Protectorate had ships large enough to ply between the Solomons and Fiji before the Second World War, when the headquarters of the Western Pacific High Commission was in Suva.

Fiji had no ships serving other islands in the Pacific as this service was provided by the Union Steam Ship Company. Fiji was also well served by overseas lines when they called at Suva and Lautoka on the way to and from the USA, Europe and Australasia.

The need for a shipping line to service the South Pacific was voiced soon after the region came together under the South Pacific Commission. The thrust, however, was provided by PIPA—the Pacific Islands Producers' Association—which had come into being as a result of discriminatory prices paid by New Zealand Fruit Distributors and succeeded in obtaining universal 'Free on Board' prices.

During this period there was a much-publicised photograph of three small, naked Fijian boys on the bank of the Wainimala River, facing the camera with their hands covering their genitals, with the caption 'No, we have no bananas'. PIPA's great effort came to naught when the blackleaf streak disease annihilated the region's banana industry. Fortunately our constituencies did not demand that we dramatise the situation by imitating the three boys on the river bank!

However, regional leaders' aspirations for a shipping service were not diminished, and a joint regional shipping company was established at the Nuku'alofa PIPA conference in 1971. Once the company was formed, the political leaders heaved a sigh of relief and wished the new venture calm seas, a fair wind and a prosperous future.

Our wish was not to be realised. Soon the line sailed into rough seas and was in danger of sinking. Fortunately, many capable hands took turns at bailing it out. The one I admired most, although our relations were initially not quite cordial, was Harry Julian. He acquainted me with the difficulties that the shipping line faced and explained that the main problem was the cost of hiring containers. I promised that I would do all that I could to help.

As chairman of the ministerial meeting of ACP/EEC I proposed that the EEC help our shipping line with a cash donation of ECU 4 million. My friend Claude Cheysson, who was in charge of development in the EEC Secretariat, strongly supported our application and, I believe, the regional shipping venture known as the Pacific Forum Line is now sailing the high seas with flying colours.

Preface

TWENTY YEARS AGO the fortunes of the Pacific Forum Line were a hotly contested political issue, regularly reviewed in the media. Today, unless you are directly involved with trade to the Pacific Islands, it is unlikely that you would know much about it. This reflects success. Despite a shaky start, the Pacific Forum Line has survived as a company and developed into a unique expression of the region's identity.

Peter Kiely, the New Zealand director, was conscious of the effort many Pacific leaders had put into the establishment of the line and seized on the twenty-year commemoration as a time to produce a record of its struggles, frustrations and achievements. He approached Dr Jock Phillips of the Historical Branch of the Department of Internal Affairs and they developed a project which has been supported by PFL's directors and staff, particularly the chairman, Taniela (Dan) Tufui, of Tonga, whose association with Pacific shipping pre-dates the formation of the Forum Line.

This brief account of the line's history has relied heavily on the records of the New Zealand Ministry of Foreign Affairs and Trade and the Australian Department of Foreign Affairs and Trade. These have been augmented by Forum Line archives, other New Zealand government department files and Forum Secretariat resources. The Australian High Commission in New Zealand facilitated access to Australian Department of Foreign Affairs and Trade records, assisted in Australia by Christopher Taylor of the Historical Documents Branch and Derek Montague of the Office of Pacific Island Affairs.

A considerable number of individuals have contributed to this project. My thanks go to His Excellency Ratu Sir Kamisese Mara, Taniela Tufui, Frances Hong Tiy, Ormond Eyre, John Townsend (Forum Secretariat), Gordon Dewsnap, Rod Gates, Michael Hirschfeld, Harry Julian, Peter Kiely, Don MacKay, John MacLennan, Ken Piddington and Gordon Shroff for their recollections. Thanks also to Graeme Eskrigge of the Ministry of Foreign Affairs and Trade, who arranged access to ministry files, David Harper of the Ministry of Transport for his help in viewing its records and Wellington Harbour Master Mike Pryce.

I am grateful to Gavin McLean, Ian McGibbon, Gordon Shroff, Peter Kiely, John MacLennan and Harry Julian, who read parts of the manuscript and whose insights were of great value. Staff at National Archives and the National Library have also given valuable assistance, as have Colin Amodeo of Christchurch and Nigel Kirby of Lyttelton.

Tony Nightingale
Wellington, 1998

Author's Note: Currency Relativities

The Pacific Forum Line is a child of the Pacific. Its earnings and expenses are in all Pacific currencies as well as United States dollars. Since the relativities between these currencies have fluctuated wildly over the twenty years of the line's existence it is impossible to convert values to one currency. I have therefore specified currencies quoted in original sources.

Abbreviations

ACP	African, Caribbean and Pacific Group
AIDAB	Australian International Development Aid Bureau
AJHR	*Appendix to the Journals of the House of Representatives*
ANL	Australian National Line
APIL	A consortium including Papua New Guinea Shipping Corporation Ltd, New Guinea Australia Line Ltd and Australia-West Pacific Line (PNG) Pty Limited
ATL	Alexander Turnbull Library
CCS	Chief Container Services (Swires)
CFTC	Commonwealth Fund for Technical Co-operation
CGM	Compagnie Générale Maritime
CHOGM	Commonwealth Heads of Government Meeting
CINL	Cook Islands National Line
ECU	European Currency Unit
EIB	European Investment Bank
FAST	Forum ANL Shipping and Transport Agency
ITF	International Transport Workers' Federation
LCL	Less than Container Load
MERT	Ministry of External Relations and Trade
MFAT	Ministry of Foreign Affairs and Trade
MV	Motor Vessel
ODA	Overseas Development Aid
OECD	Organisation for Economic Co-operation and Development
P&O	Peninsula and Oriental Shipping Company
PFL	Pacific Forum Line
PIPA	Pacific Islands Producers' Association
RORO	roll-on, roll-off
SCONZ	Shipping Corporation of New Zealand
SPARTECA	South Pacific Regional Trade and Economic Co-operation Agreement
SPEC	South Pacific Bureau for Economic Co-operation
TEU	Twenty-foot Equivalent Unit (twenty feet being the length of a standard container)
UMS	Union Maritime Services
UNESCAP	United Nations Economic and Social Commission for Asia and the Pacific

Contents

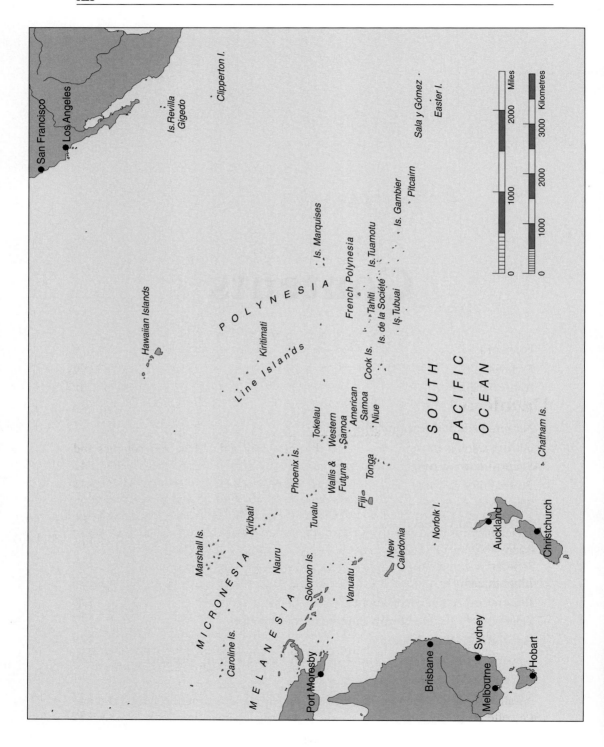

Introduction: The South Pacific Forum

Decolonisation

THE CURRENT South Pacific Forum members were all closely associated with colonial powers from the nineteenth century onwards. Most were colonies and most have gained independence in the period since World War II. This shared experience is an important factor in the Forum's perspective on a wide range of issues. Colonial powers in the Pacific have generally had a sense of responsibility towards their colonies even after the granting of independence. Moreover, the former administering power was in a unique position to understand the hybrid political systems established in the colonial period.

Populations of British extraction were established in Australia from the late eighteenth century and in New Zealand from early in the nineteenth. The original inhabitants, Aboriginals and Maori, became British subjects in 1788 and 1840 respectively. Antipodean European populations were quickly granted a considerable degree of autonomy and developed standards of living comparable with Britain.

For Pacific Island states the pattern was different. Colonisation came later, the indigenous population remained predominant, living standards differed from those of the colonial powers, and independence was not attained until after 1960.

Britain offered to administer Fiji in 1874 and, at various times between 1884 and 1906, offered protection to Papua, the Solomon Islands, the Cook Islands, the

Gilbert and Ellice Islands, Niue, Tonga and, in association with France, the New
Hebrides. Between 1884 and 1899 Germany annexed New Guinea and its offshore
islands, Samoa* and Nauru, and also acquired the Mariana, Caroline and Marshall
Islands. The Americans acquired Guam as a result of the Spanish–American war
and obtained American Samoa, with its deep-water harbour at Pago Pago, under
a trilateral treaty with Britain and Germany.

After World War I Germany was displaced as a colonial power by Japan in
Micronesia, by Australia in Melanesia and by New Zealand in Samoa. Nauru's rich
phosphate deposits were exploited by a joint Australian, New Zealand and British
commission, although the key administering power was Australia. The tiny islands
of Midway, Wake, Howland, Baker, Jarvis and Johnston were later claimed by the
United States, while Canton and Enderbury went to Britain, largely to serve as
stepping stones for early trans-Pacific air services. Only Tonga remained self-
governing and independent.[1]

State	Status of Sovereignty	Self-Government
American Samoa	Territory of USA	Substantial
Cook Islands	Free Association NZ (1965)	Total
Federated States of Micronesia	Free Association US (1986)	Total
Fiji	Independent (1970)	Total
French Polynesia	Territory of France	Substantial
Guam	Territory of USA	Substantial
Kiribati	Independent (1979)	Total
Marshall Islands	Free Association USA (1986)	Total
Nauru	Independent (1968)	Total
New Caledonia	Territory of France	Substantial
Niue	Free Association NZ (1974)	Total
Northern Mariana Islands	Commonwealth of USA	Substantial
Palau (Belau)	Independent (1994)	Total
Papua New Guinea	Independent (1975)	Total
Pitcairn	Dependency of UK	Limited
Samoa	Independent (1962)	Total
Solomon Islands	Independent (1978)	Total
Tokelau	Territory of NZ[2]	Limited
Tonga	Independent	Total
Tuvalu	Independent (1978)	Total
Vanuatu	Independent (1980)	Total
Wallis and Futuna	Territory of France	Substantial[3]

*Prior to 1997 Samoa was called Western Samoa.

Decolonisation in the Pacific is still unfolding but has been neither as vehement nor as violent as African or Caribbean independence movements. Most Forum countries retain a positive relationship with their former administering powers, who at times contribute considerable aid to the region. For example, Australia assists Papua New Guinea while New Zealand assists Niue and the Cook Islands. The Pacific Forum includes more than a dozen members of the British Commonwealth.

Only France and the United States still maintain significant territories in the area. The French possessions, New Caledonia and French Polynesia, are dominated by populations of French extraction who increasingly determine domestic and trade policy and seem keen to maintain a close association with France. Indigenous populations display a more ambivalent response to continued French involvement. The continuing association of the United States with the Commonwealth of the Northern Mariana Islands and American Samoa appears to be mutually agreeable, largely because no practical alternative could provide Islanders with a comparable standard of living. The same could be said of New Zealand's relationship with Tokelau and Britain's with its last South Pacific territory, Pitcairn Island.

The form of most current governments of Forum countries mirrors that of their colonial power and many are parliamentary, reflecting the strong British influence in the region. However, while many Island institutions were modelled on those of the colonial power, the similarities should not be overstated. Pacific peoples have adapted usages to reflect their own traditional values and much government is personalised, with considerations such as kinship and status often being very important.

Regional Organisations

The first Pacific regional organisation was the South Pacific Commission, established in 1947 as a result of the 1944 Canberra Pact to give those with Pacific interests a say in post-war international re-organisation. Its purpose was to link the colonial powers with Australia and New Zealand, two independent former colonies which had themselves assumed colonial responsibilities. From the 1960s, newly independent Pacific states were encouraged to join but the agendas were controlled and 'political issues', particularly those associated with independence, were avoided. Moreover, the distribution of money was determined by the former colonial powers, which the independent states perceived as a tool for rewarding those who 'toed the line'. Emerging Pacific nations joined the South Pacific Commission but increasingly felt constrained. A push for a new forum came particularly from the Fijian Prime Minister, Ratu Sir Kamisese Mara, who pressed for the formation of a distinct international body where issues affecting Island nations could be discussed.

New Zealand and Australia supported the formation of such an organisation, with New Zealand facilitating the process by providing the venue for the inaugural meeting. The first South Pacific Forum was held in Wellington in April 1971, attended by Samoa, Tonga, Nauru, Fiji, the Cook Islands, Australia and New Zealand. All had a common 'British' background and a relatively smooth and uncontested road to independence.[4]

Nine further countries have since joined the Forum—Niue and Papua New Guinea (both 1975), Tuvalu (1978), Kiribati (pronounced Kiribas, 1979), Vanuatu (1981), the Marshall Islands (1986), the Federated States of Micronesia, the Commonwealth of the Northern Mariana Islands and Palau (all 1987).[5]

Britain was the major colonial power in the Pacific. In 1953 Queen Elizabeth II, accompanied by Ratu Sir Lala Sukuna, the Duke of Edinburgh and the Governor of Fiji arrived at Albert Park for the Fijian ceremonies of welcome.

Political and Economic Conditions

The Australian and New Zealand economies differed from those of the Island nations. They were developed, with a standard of living at the upper end of the OECD scale, and their considerable administrative infrastructure included air and shipping links with the rest of the world. Since both countries were still administering Pacific islands, Nauru initially took the stance that this should exclude them from membership of the South Pacific Forum. However, Fiji's desire to include them prevailed and it was clear from the outset that their role would be to facilitate the development of a body to enhance regional interaction and security. To be effective the Forum would need the financial and political support of Canberra and Wellington.[6]

There is a considerable development gap between the large and small Pacific nations. This has increased rather than decreased in the post-colonial period. Papua New Guinea, Fiji, the Solomon Islands and Vanuatu have extensive, relatively under-developed agricultural or mineral resources whose sensible development can be used to raise their populations' incomes and standards of living. Tonga, Samoa, the Cook Islands, the Federated States of Micronesia, the Marshall Islands and Palau have more limited resources. Throughout the last twenty years large injections of aid, external payments and remittances have allowed them to maintain standards of living above those sustainable by their productivity. Even with development, large amounts of outside assistance seem likely to remain important.

Kiribati and Tuvalu are among the least developed countries in the Pacific, with few natural resources or export commodities. Currently, remittances from expatriates are very important to their economies, while one hope for development stems from their large marine areas. Both countries are heavily dependent on aid and are likely to remain so in the near future.

Nauru is the only Pacific country not to receive aid. However, income from its rich phosphate deposits is destined to end in the near future, and Nauru will need to ensure that it is not visited by the problems of the resource-poor states.[7]

Organisational Development

The nature and focus of the South Pacific Forum have changed as it has grown. At first it was primarily a south-west Pacific and Polynesian organisation. By the 1990s its membership had diversified, with a strong representation of Melanesian and Micronesian interests. In the early period, Forum meetings were characterised by consensus, a considerable degree of informality, and remarkable unanimity. However, there have been significant divisions which have created a need for increased formality. Melanesian members have strongly supported indigenous Kanaks in New Caledonia in their desire for independence from France, and have encouraged Kanak representatives to attend Forum meetings as unofficial observers. At the same time they have resisted the inclusion of non-independent United States or French Island governments and questioned Australian and New Zealand involvement. Polynesian members have been generally ambivalent towards nationalist issues and still value highly the link with Australia and New Zealand.

The Forum has a considerable number of subsidiary organisations and has supported the formation of many independent bodies such as the South Pacific Regional Shipping Council (1974), the South Pacific Regional Civil Aviation Council (1976), the Forum Fisheries Agency (1979), the Regional Committee on Trade (1979) and the South Pacific Telecommunications Development Programme (1983). It has also endorsed the establishment of the South Pacific Applied Geoscience Commission (1989) and the South Pacific Regional Environmental Programme (1980). Since the varied nature and status of these bodies led to co-ordination difficulties, the Forum established in 1988 the South Pacific Organisations Co-ordinating Committee. However, the South Pacific Commission declined an invitation to join and the respective roles of the Forum and the Commission remain unclear.[8]

The Pacific Forum Line was formed in 1977. It is unique amongst regional governmental organisations because it is an operating company whose primary objective is to make a profit for shareholders. All South Pacific Forum members are entitled to join and there are currently twelve shareholders, namely the Cook Islands, Fiji, Kiribati, Marshall Islands, Nauru, New Zealand, Niue, Papua New Guinea, Samoa, Solomon Islands, Tonga and Tuvalu.[9] Australia, Palau, the Federated States of Micronesia and Vanuatu are members of the Forum but not shareholders in the line.

The Forum Secretariat logo.

CHAPTER ONE

Nationalism and Regionalism

B Y THE END of the nineteenth century the most significant Pacific shipowner was the Union Steam Ship Company of New Zealand, which had begun its Pacific service in 1881. It had dominated trade for nearly a century but, by the 1960s, had long since been taken over by the English P&O Line.[10] However, the Union Steam Ship Company identity remained and operated a New Zealand-managed passenger and freight service over much of the Pacific. Several Australian companies also served the region, while Fiji was directly served by European lines.[11] A number of larger operators stopped off in the Pacific as part of their Australasia–America and Australasia–Europe trade.

The Union Company's first Pacific service had been subsidised by the New Zealand government, but once it proved profitable the grant was withdrawn.[12] Pacific services remained generally viable until they began to make consistent losses in the early 1960s. There were several reasons for this: the serious decline of the banana trade due to disease, stiff competition from South American fruit producers and increasing passenger air travel. There was also uncertainty surrounding the Union Company's commitment to the region. This led some producers to seek alternative services, which all too often proved unreliable.

Island leaders' anxiety over the Union Company's commitment to the Pacific was compounded when, on 1 January 1972, Australia's Thomas Nationwide Transport and a consortium of New Zealand interests purchased the Union Company from

1

P&O.[13] The Union Company had not been performing for its English parent and needed significant restructuring in a bid to regain profitability.

Part of the problem was that P&O had never thoroughly integrated the Union Company into its organisation, despite the fact that this might have provided greater efficiencies in both operations. New Zealand management generally ran the trans-Tasman, Pacific and Indian routes and, in the inter-war period, created healthy cashflows for the benefit of the whole group. Post-war, the New Zealand operation had great difficulty in containing costs, both onshore and at sea. Shipping had become a high-cost industry and local shippers were critical of the Union Company's inability to contain its costs.[14] By the 1960s the New Zealand operation was in poor shape, the company having neglected the development of its infrastructure, particularly in the Pacific.

At the time of the 1971 Commission of Inquiry into New Zealand Shipping the Union Company operated two conventional vessels on the Pacific trade. These were the *Taveuni*, a refrigerated and general cargo vessel of 2830 tons, and the *Waimate*, a general cargo vessel of 5154 tons. They were complemented by the *Tofua*, a passenger-cargo vessel which called at all the major island ports in the central Pacific.

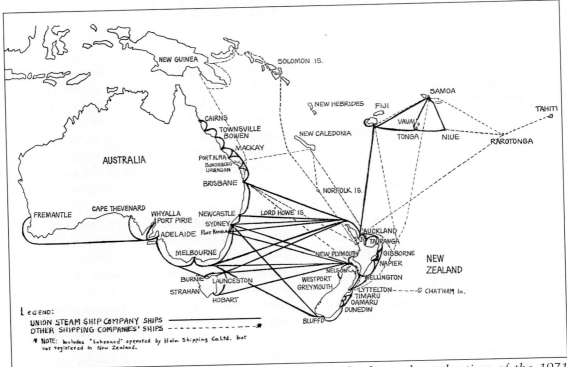

This hand-drawn map shows ports served by New Zealand vessels at the time of the 1971 Commission of Inquiry into New Zealand Shipping.

The international development of unitised, containerised shipping was well under way by the mid-1960s. Although the Union Company's Pacific services remained conventional throughout the 1960s, its vessels were due for replacement in the early- to mid-1970s. However, by 1971 the company was poorly placed to make the necessary capital investment.

Containerised shipping did not just mean the unitisation of cargo. It was also necessary to purchase new, larger and more expensive ships, to invest considerably in onshore facilities and to reduce crew. Such drastic change was bound to provoke conflict with the maritime unions. It was only after the sale of the Union Company by P&O that the new Australasian management could address what, by 1971, had become pressing issues.

Early in 1972, the Union Company's new management was considering the introduction of containerised shipping on the Pacific run and had decided to cease operating the passenger service, which duly ended on 4 June 1973.[15] The company's conventional freighters were replaced by the small, chartered Tarros class container vessel *Union South Pacific* which traded the New Zealand–Fiji–Samoa–Tonga route, although it was always intended that this service would require two such vessels. In order to gain maximum flexibility at less developed ports, the *Union South Pacific* was loaded and discharged by a combination of truck and trailer units driven up the ship's ramp and stowed by the ship's gantry crane.

A subsidiary of the Union Company, the Holm Shipping Company, ran a conventional chartered freighter, the *Luhesand*, on the New Zealand–Rarotonga–Papeete route,[16] where it was in competition with the New Zealand government passenger-cargo vessel, *Moana Roa*, on the New Zealand–Rarotonga leg. This service also returned a loss which severely compromised the Holm Company's profitability.

New Zealand labour costs were high by international standards and port turn-around was very slow, yet shipping lines and successive New Zealand governments had been reluctant to take significant action to reduce costs since this might have led to industrial disharmony. Ships on Pacific runs were crewed by New Zealand seamen and the Union Company's interests were perceived by many in emergent Island states as being closely associated with those of the New Zealand government—even when successive governments attempted to dispel this perception.[17]

The Union Company was unfavourably identified with the colonial administration in the minds of many Island leaders and there was a widespread desire for a new start, especially since the Union Company was at times less than sympathetic towards Pacific sensibilities. After the 1971 Fiji dock strike, management increased freight rates to Fiji by 15 per cent to recover the extra costs of stevedoring at Lautoka and Suva.[18] This action, which was not matched by other Pacific operators, upset Island governments, many of whom felt that they were being reminded by the Union Company that it was predominant in regional shipping.

The Pacific Trade and the Introduction of Containerisation

Established within the context of Pacific Island moves towards independence, the Pacific Forum Line was also shaped by contemporary developments in international transport. At the time of the 1971 Commission of Inquiry into New Zealand Shipping there were no definitive statistics on Pacific trade, but several observations may be made on the distinctive nature of operating vessels in the region. The trade had become heavily one-way: Island produce exports had declined and exports from Australia and New Zealand predominated. Empty return voyages meant a greater unit cost of freight to the Islands.

The passenger-cargo vessel *Tofua* served the region but the passenger trade was under threat from airlines. There was a widespread impression that the freight trade was not generally profitable and that the Union Company continued its service out of tradition. Australian cargo was carried by the Karlander Shipping Company Pty Ltd, which called at Tonga and Samoa on their United States route. Fiji was served by Karlander and Compagnie Générale Maritime (CGM) en route to the USA and Europe.[19]

Pacific Island independence and the establishment of the South Pacific Forum coincided with a period of considerable instability in the shipping industry. A feature of the 1960s and 1970s was massive cost increases, particularly on conventional vessels. Some 60 to 70 per cent could be attributed to higher labour costs. Companies had little choice but to pass these on because, for over a century, they had been unable to make any substantial reduction in labour requirements while using traditional cargo-handling methods.[20] From the late 1950s a few shipping companies began to control costs with the adoption of roll-on, roll-off, bulk carriage and container systems.

However, container-based and specialist bulk systems were much more capital-intensive than their conventional predecessors and required considerable infra-structural development before the savings could be passed on. As efficiencies were much greater on high-volume routes, containerisation was first introduced on ships carrying cargo between Europe and the USA and a little later from Europe to Australia and New Zealand.

On low-volume routes such as the South Pacific where port facilities were often rudimentary, containerisation needed to be adapted. Vessels had to be smaller, suited to the scale of trade, self-sustaining and flexible. They had to carry their own ramps and cranes and have a roll-on, roll-off capacity. Such vessels were expensive to build and their operating costs were high compared with the large and simple cellular vessels on major trade routes.

By the 1960s Pacific trade was conducted mainly by the Union Company and, to a lesser extent, by Burns Philp Ltd of Australia. Both had difficulty making their services pay with ageing, conventional fleets and were aware that they would need to invest in new ships. Burns Philp, whose fleet was due for renewal in the 1970s, sold its interest in the trade and Karlander, a Norwegian-based firm, became the main Australian shipper in the Pacific by 1971.[21]

The Union Company vessels, built in the 1950s, were also due for renewal.[22] However, as Australasian labour costs were high, the Pacific service was unprofitable and trans-Tasman trade was marginal, the London-based owners, P&O, decided to sell the Union Company rather than reinvest.

National Shipping Companies

By 1971 the Union Company's role in the Pacific was further threatened by the shipping operations of two Island governments, Tonga and Nauru.

In 1970 the Tongan Shipping Agency operated two ships on overseas runs. The first, the *Aonui*, had been purchased in 1959 by the Tongan Producers' Board to trade between Fiji and Tonga. In November 1963 the Tongan Copra Board purchased the *Niuvakai*, with the intention of transporting coconuts from Tonga to Pago Pago. When this trade did not eventuate the ship was put on the Tonga–Fiji–Australia route in direct competition with a service introduced by the Union Company two years earlier.[23] In May 1972, these shipping interests, which had previously been managed by the Tongan Shipping Agency, were formed into a national line—the Pacific Navigation Company of Tonga Ltd.[24] Later that year the *Niuvakai* was withdrawn and replaced by the *Tauloto*.

Phosphate-rich Nauru had also purchased ships in the 1960s and, by April 1971, operated three conventional freighter and passenger-freight vessels—the *Eigamoya*, *Rosie D*, and *Enna G*[25]—on the Australia–Nauru run and even for cruises. The Nauruans had plans to purchase further ships and were prepared to commit a considerable amount of capital into the development of a line. To crew the vessels, the company hired from outside Nauru, particularly from Tonga.

Tonga and Nauru worked independently to develop their shipping interests but both made considerable losses and the viability of their operations was brought into question, at least by other shipowners. However, there were various suggestions from Island leaders that these assets should be used as the basis of a regional shipping line. In February 1973, representatives of the Pacific Navigation Company Ltd and Nauru Pacific Line met to examine the possibility of establishing a regional carrier based on their fleets, but by this time there was growing support for wider regional involvement.[26]

The Pacific Islands Producers' Association

The move to form a regional shipping line was part of a wider push for the development of regional autonomy. It was only with the advent of a sense of regional identity, cemented by the formation of Pacific organisations, that co-ordination became practicable. At the centre of the call for a regional shipping line was the Pacific Islands Producers' Association (PIPA) which had been established in 1965 by the Fijian and Samoan governments and banana growers, who were soon joined by their Tongan, Cook Island and Niuean counterparts.

Transport costs for Pacific Island agricultural exports were considerable since they were all high-bulk, low-value cargoes. As highly perishable bananas in particular needed to be moved as soon as possible after harvest, PIPA officials quickly began to put pressure on the Union Company to improve its schedules and service.

The timing was important. PIPA, the first regional organisation driven by Island interests, arose at a time when South Pacific nations were gaining independence. It was natural that the organisation would come to embody emergent nationalism.

Moreover, the commercial operation of PIPA's members mirrored the wider post-colonial relationship. Island banana growers had one major outlet through New Zealand Fruit Distributors—a government-regulated body responsible for supplying bananas and pineapples to the entire New Zealand market. One of PIPA's most notable successes was to achieve a universal 'Free on Board' price for all Island suppliers, regardless of how far away the supplier was from New Zealand.[27]

Nevertheless, PIPA did not wield significant power in the banana market. Island producers had considerable difficulty competing with Ecuadorean growers, while the 'Free on Board' price was only possible within the context of the Fruit Distributors' monopoly. By 1971, Island politicians and business leaders were frustrated by repeated freight rate increases and the irregularity of services. It was in this context that they called for the establishment of a joint regional shipping company at the April Nuku'alofa PIPA conference.

COOK   ISLANDS

PRIMARY PRODUCE MARKETING BOARD
SOLE EXPORTERS · CITRUS FRUITS · BANANAS · PINEAPPLES · COPRA OF COOK ISLANDS

The Cook Islands Primary Produce Marketing Board was one of the four main producer boards in the South Pacific.

New Zealand Government Support

There had often been governmental involvement in the provision of shipping services to the Pacific. New Zealand in particular had long been supportive. In the nineteenth century this had often been to secure mail services. In the twentieth century subsidisation became part of what it saw as its colonial duty, particularly to the Cook Islands, Niue and Tokelau. The exact nature of this duty was ill-defined and, when a debate about responsibility for shipping developed at the time of Cook Islands independence, there was no clear understanding. As late as the 1960s the Cook Islands viewpoint was that Richard John Seddon (New Zealand Premier at the turn of the century) had promised them a regular shipping service in return for ceding sovereignty.[28]

However, it would appear that no such service had been established and the run was taken up by commercial operators sometimes subsidised by the government. The New Zealand government did offer a service from 1936 onwards, using first the *Matua* and then the *Maui Pomare*, but this competed with private operators until March 1961 when the Union Company withdrew its vessels.[29] The government-owned *Maui Pomare* was in turn replaced by the *Moana Roa*, which continued in service until 1974.

PIPA representatives made a courtesy call on New Zealand Prime Minister Keith Holyoake in 1968 after negotiations with New Zealand Fruit Distributors chairman Sir Harvey Turner. From the left, Laufili Time (Minister of Agriculture, Samoa), Ratu Mara (Prime Minister, Fiji), Keith Holyoake, Mahe Tupouniua (Minister of Finance and Deputy Prime Minister, Tonga) and Eddie Stehlin (secretary to the delegation).

New Zealand support for shipping to the Cook Islands changed considerably after the Cooks gained independence. In 1970 Albert Henry's government formed the Cook Islands Shipping Company in which the Island administration and Julian Holdings Ltd of Auckland held equal shares. The company initially chartered the reefer vessel *Thallo* which later had an Island crew. New Zealand maritime unions objected and the ensuing dispute was costly for the company. Eventually the unions accepted the crew on the understanding that if a larger vessel was placed on the run, a 'New Zealand' crew would replace the Cook Islanders.[30]

When development of Avatiu Harbour allowed larger vessels to call at the Cooks and freight volumes on the *Thallo* increased, the Cook Islands Shipping Company purchased the *Lorena*, a Norwegian-built conventional freighter, which ran in competition with the *Moana Roa*. The latter was a slightly older vessel and it became obvious that air travel would soon render her passenger service redundant. Both services were losing money. In an attempt to make the *Lorena* profitable, the Cook Islands Shipping Company sought New Zealand government support to re-crew with Cook Islanders rather than New Zealanders.[31]

This caused an uproar from New Zealand unionists. The National government refused to support any such move [32] and turned down a request for $164,000 to bail out the Cook Islands Shipping Company. The incoming Labour administration in New Zealand looked more favourably at supporting the Cook Islands service but

The New Zealand government vessel Maui Pomare *at anchor at Rarotonga in 1956. On a calm sea the lighters could easily take on freight. However the Pacific swell often made loading a dangerous business requiring great skill.*

emphasised that, even though it intended to withdraw the *Moana Roa*, it was not prepared to deal with a company which had considerable private share-holding.[33]

As a consequence of Prime Minister Norman Kirk's visit to Rarotonga in April 1973, New Zealand provided a loan to allow the Cook Islands to purchase the rest of the Cook Islands Shipping Company shares, wind up the company and leave the way clear for a joint venture with New Zealand. A decision had already been made to remove the *Moana Roa* from service in April 1974 and convert it to the Royal New Zealand Navy hydrographic ship. In March 1974 officials agreed to set up a joint venture based on two unitised vessels on a fortnightly schedule.[34] This took the Cook Islands service outside the auspices of any regional shipping line until the shipping industry restructuring of the late 1980s. Service under this joint venture

An official party arriving at Pukapuka in the Cook Islands from the New Zealand government vessel, Moana Roa. *The visitor was New Zealand Minister of Internal Affairs, Leon Götz.*

was provided by the *Lorena* and the *Toa Moana*, which were soon replaced with the small unitised vessels, *Fetu Moana* and *Tiare Moana*.

In the period after World War II, successive New Zealand governments had generally not assisted commercial operators on Pacific routes but did, from time to time, offer subsidies towards the development of a route. In December 1965 the Holyoake government had provided the Holm Shipping Company with NZ$72,000 for nine voyages to establish a trade to Noumea and Norfolk Island. A further NZ$30,000 was given in 1967 but the subsidy was then discontinued and the service ended. In 1970 the New Zealand Export Line received a $76,000 subsidy for a route from New Zealand to Honiara, Kieta, Rabaul, Lae and Port Moresby. However, this venture incurred considerable losses and was terminated a year later. Both services were subsequently provided by the Pacific Forum Line.

Making a profit from shipping in the Pacific was more difficult in the 1960s than earlier. The Union Company's decade of loss-making led its new management to consider requesting a subsidy for its Pacific services. The head of Thomas Nationwide Transport, Sir Peter Abeles, stated in February 1971 that, although he was not a believer in subsidies, should the government request the Union Company to run a service with a subsidy being made available, he would accept it. The Holm Shipping Company went further and requested a subsidy for the *Luhesand* on the Rarotonga–Papeete route, but this was turned down by the New Zealand government.[35]

The Toa Moana *in Lyttelton Harbour in 1978.*

The New Zealand Maritime Unions

If the Union Company had formerly been supreme in Pacific trade, then the New Zealand maritime unions dominated the industrial climate. Union Company ships had traditionally been crewed by New Zealand seamen and the practice remained, despite the fact that New Zealand award wages were considerably above international rates and vastly superior to what Island seamen could expect. While the Union Company might have wished to hire cheaper Island crews, this was politically untenable and would have caused widespread industrial disruption.

The New Zealand Seamen's Union had consistently expressed its opposition to foreign (non-New Zealand) crews. Fintan Patrick Walsh had stated the policy succinctly in response to a 1931 visit by a Japanese-manned merchant ship:

> We have no objection to the Japanese; they are workers, exploited just the same as we are. The point at issue is that the standards we have built up are undermined by the invasion of ships with crews on wages and conditions much lower than ours . . . But of course the shipping barons wouldn't bring them all this way if they had to pay them higher wages . . . If we can show them what good wages and conditions can be won by strong unions, then we'll be striking a blow for Japanese workers as well as ourselves.[36]

New Zealand maritime unions opposed foreign-owned vessels operating on what they saw as their 'traditional' routes—which included the Pacific. They could be expected to take industrial action against any foreign vessel which did not employ crews enjoying union wages and conditions. The unions would probably have accepted a foreign vessel which paid New Zealand wages and was on a direct trade between her home country and New Zealand. However, if the vessel were to trade in other countries en route to or from New Zealand, this would be rejected as cross-trading.

The significance of the union position for Island-crewed vessels was considerable. If Island-crewed vessels were not fully owned and operated by Islanders and offering wages at New Zealand levels, or if they engaged in cross-trading, then the unions usually took industrial action. This had been a perennial problem for Island-manned vessels. In September 1971 the motor vessel *Thallo* was prevented from beginning a regular service on the Lyttelton–Suva run. The Seamen's Union objected to the introduction of this service by a non-New Zealand crew, even though the same vessel had previously traded with an Island crew between Auckland and Rarotonga.[37]

The *Enna G* Dispute

The Union Company inadvertently provoked industrial conflict over Pacific Island access to New Zealand trade when, in June 1973, it removed the *Tofua* from her run. The Nauru Pacific Line attempted to pick up the service using the *Enna G*. The Nauruans widely advertised the advent of the new service as a replacement for the *Tofua*, which alerted the New Zealand union movement to the possibility that a Nauruan ship with a non-New Zealand crew was about to take over a service previously crewed by its members.

In May 1973 the Nauru Pacific Line sent the *Enna G* to the Wellington floating dock to prepare her for service, which was scheduled to begin from Auckland on 3 June 1973. However, the agents, Seatrans of Auckland, were told that watersiders and tally clerks at Auckland would not work the ship because the Fijian crew did not have International Transport Workers' Federation (ITF) wages and conditions.

Nauru President Hammer DeRoburt requested that the New Zealand government intervene to ensure that the ship could sail on schedule.[38] In the meantime the *Enna G* was declared black by the combined waterfront unions, who claimed that their stance was taken in response to a request for assistance from the Fijian crew. Subsequent investigations tended to support this, although the timing of the dispute gave the union an opportunity to reinforce its traditional opposition to all foreign-owned vessels. E. G. Davey, New Zealand Labour Department Secretary, emphasised this in his report to his Minister:

> I believe that underlying their actions also is their basic opposition to ships other than New Zealand-manned ones entering into the Pacific trade and, of course, the arrival of the *Enna G* coincided with the paying off of the *Tofua*.[39]

The New Zealand Labour government, which had a close association with the union movement, was unwilling to assist Hammer DeRoburt. Hemmed in, the Nauruan owners attempted to get the Fijian crew to go to sea. Exactly where they intended to go was not clear because the unions' ban on the ship meant it could not enter a New Zealand port. When the crew refused to obey the order, attempts were made to sack them. This was resisted by the New Zealand unions. In a series of meetings, both sides remained entrenched. The crew were eventually dismissed on 12 June but remained in Wellington as guests of the combined waterfront unions.

Running the headline 'Enna G rides out storm of Pacific Island power politics', the New Zealand *National Business Review* claimed that the writing had been on the wall since the Pacific Forum had endorsed the concept of a regional shipping line two years previously, and correctly predicted the need for a political solution:

> It's not much use to them to get the Fijians back on board, even with major reductions in their original claims, if the ship is only going to run into a trade union brick wall when it arrives in Auckland to begin the service and there's a demand for a New Zealand crew.
>
> The Nauruans' whole object has been to get the New Zealand government involved in an attempt to break the New Zealand stranglehold on some Pacific routes.
>
> For this reason the Nauruans have some incentive not to settle the argument over the Fijians but rather to use them in an attempt to embarrass the New Zealand unions.
>
> The New Zealand government has tried to remain out of the argument and its only position is that there could be reason for a Pacific conference on the question of shipping services run by Islands Governments.[40]

Despite repeated attempts at mediation by Labour Minister Hugh Watt, the Nauruans remained determined either to place the ship on the former *Tofua* route or to have her sit in Wellington Harbour as an embodiment of Pacific Island aspirations.[41] They could have moved the vessel—the maritime unions were happy to see the *Enna G* sail from New Zealand as long as there was no attempt to set up the proposed service.[42] The Nauruan response to the failed negotiations was to place a full-page advertisement in major New Zealand newspapers appealing directly for public support.

The *Pacific Islands Monthly* couched its description of the dispute in nationalistic terms:

> For the *Enna G* is no simple shipping dispute. It is the independent nations of the South Pacific versus the metropolitan powers for a place in the sun.
>
> The principle is: Do the sovereign South Pacific states not have the right to operate their own ships, to employ their own men and on their own conditions or to call any place else whose government gives them authority to call?

The *Enna G* finally left New Zealand on 21 September 1973. As a consequence of the dispute, New Zealand Prime Minister Norman Kirk offered to convene a conference at Waitangi on Pacific shipping with a view to facilitating Pacific Island participation.

Invitations to the Waitangi conference included many Pacific Island Ministers, a cross-section of shipowners, and representatives of all the major maritime unions.[43] There was one major omission—the Australian government. New Zealand officials believed that this issue was of little relevance to the Australians, partly because of their limited involvement in Pacific shipping and partly because Australian unions did not have any objection to cross-trading by foreign-owned ships.[44] Australian Department of Foreign Affairs officials were happy for the conference to go ahead in their absence, with the reservation that they did not want it to overshadow the regional Ministers of Labour conference scheduled for Sydney on 30 October.[45]

Enna G Rides out storm of Pacific Islands power politics

Industrial Correspondent

The Enna G *remained at Wellington from June to September 1973.*

The Waitangi Conference

The conference took place from 25 to 27 October 1973. The symbolism of the Waitangi site, where the British Crown had signed a treaty with Maori, was important for many who attended. In his keynote speech Norman Kirk made it clear that his sympathies were with the Island governments. He drew a comparison between the Islands' desire to influence Pacific shipping and New Zealand's move to set up the Shipping Corporation of New Zealand.

Norman Kirk.

No one, least of all those nations which have been traditional suppliers of shipping to us, has suggested that it is improper for New Zealand to develop its own shipping service. I believe that we must in our turn adopt the same attitude to others who seek to have an interest in their own shipping services. ...

... We all want our countries to become more prosperous; we all want to help the Island countries to develop their human resources, their skills and natural resources of their islands; we all want better and expanding shipping services in the region; we all want seamen and shipping operators to get a good deal; we all want the South Pacific countries to co-operate more closely in all fields; from this basis of agreement we can all go forward.[46]

Kirk's move to emphasise similarities in the New Zealand and Island post-colonial positions was a shrewd ploy designed to facilitate union co-operation.[47] He argued that New Zealand seamen would gain job opportunities from the establishment of the Shipping Corporation of New Zealand and so could afford to let Islanders onto the Pacific routes. Conference chairman Eddie Isbey reiterated this message to the Federation of Labour and the maritime unions.

At the same time those Islanders who manned vessels coming to New Zealand had to be paid in accordance with ITF rates. It was hoped that this would be acceptable to the New Zealand unionists. Australian unions had accepted an agreement which allowed Pacific Island seamen trained at the Gilbert and Ellice Islands' Training School to work on routes including Australia. It was hoped that the New Zealand unions could be encouraged to accept a similar arrangement. This was vital if there was to be any chance of a regional shipping line because all the preparatory economic surveys had shown that any other system, including using Fiji as an entrepot, was unlikely to be viable.[48]

Most of the work of the conference was in committee and the joint communiqué spoke in generalities. Union representatives recognised 'the right of Island governments to play a more active role in the development of Island and regional shipping, to invest their own capital and to employ their own citizens at all levels in whatever organisations were established, and to carry a significant part of the trade their markets generate.' The communiqué also re-stated the South Pacific Forum's intention to continue investigating the formation of a regional line.[49]

Although the Waitangi conference was useful and became a constant reference point, there was no overall agreement. Part of its authority no doubt stemmed from the fact that the communiqué was open to widely varying interpretations.

Only the Tongan delegation leader, Taniela (Dan) Tufui, publicly addressed the New Zealand union intransigence in the *Enna G* dispute.

> NZ workers lashed out blindly and violently caught their fellow workers in the Islands full in the face.
> … reasons offered were that the Islanders were trespassing on traditional routes or cross-trading. However, the Island people did not want to prohibit New Zealand ships from trading with Tonga and other island groups. All they wanted was the right to enter into trade and at rates of pay they could afford.[50]

New Zealand Federation of Labour secretary Jim Knox argued that the Seamen's Union was very concerned by Mr Tufui's remarks, and emphasised that Norman Kirk had set the tone of the conference as 'Let's talk about the future'. What he did not reveal was the maritime unions' likely response to future visits.

Noel Holmes of the *Auckland Star* was doubtful whether the Island leaders' enthusiasm for a regional shipping line was soundly based, although he suggested that it was no more irrational than New Zealand's determination to form the Shipping Corporation. His remarks were widely reported in the Pacific:

> The Pacific Islands have a vague dream about a regional shipping line of their own. And they have the same ambitions as we have. Maybe they will lose money (Mr. D. C. Jury of the Union Steam Ship Company spelt it out to the conference that there was no financial joy in Pacific shipping) but at least they will fulfil a dream, just as we are.[51]

The New Zealand government had worked hard to ensure that the Waitangi conference went smoothly. Preparations had included a series of meetings between ministers, officials, and participants. One of the thorniest problems was the intention of the Nauruan Council to sue the New Zealand maritime unions for damages as a result of blacklisting the *Enna G.* Foreign Affairs officials persuaded Hammer DeRoburt not to file the writ before the conference but failed to deter him afterwards. It was filed in Wellington in December 1973 and the consequent case took more than a decade to resolve. It became the cause of considerable tension between unionists and the New Zealand government and was frequently revisited.[52] It was also a major obstacle to any formal agreement with the unions on cross-trading.

Proposals

At the time of the Waitangi conference it was clear there were to be considerable changes to Pacific shipping, regardless of whether a regional shipping line was formed. What follows is a brief chronological overview of the major proposals and some comment on how they interacted.

Island governments had already rejected a proposal by a San Francisco-based group—fronted by a New Zealand subsidiary, Inter Ocean (NZ) Ltd—for a Pacific container service. When the American representative, Charles Halloraker, attended the September 1971 PIPA conference at Nuku'alofa, he was told: 'Delegates at the PIPA meeting did not take kindly to ... (his) container proposition because . . . it would conflict with the regional shipping line which PIPA member governments intended setting up.'[53]

At this stage the Union Company was adamant that it had no intention of withdrawing from the Pacific.[54] Only after its sale by P&O was there any public announcement of its plans to make the service competitive and viable. David Jury, who was responsible for the Union Company's Pacific services, told New Zealand Foreign Affairs officials that, in the first nine months of 1972, the company had lost $500,000 on the service and that to break even would require a freight increase of 12 per cent. Despite its losses, the company still favoured replacing its three conventional vessels with two Tarros class container vessels and was investigating the problems of carrying bananas in containers*.

---

*Bananas perished easily. With conventional shipping, natural airflow limited ripening and maintained an appropriate humidity. The first containers reduced airflow and increased humidity, which led to unacceptable losses of fruit. It was very difficult to provide the correct freight conditions and it was not until the late 1970s that appropriate containers for tropical fruits were developed.[55]

Union Company management, recognising that Pacific shipping was risky, was prepared to reduce its equity and financial risk by allowing Tonga, Samoa and Fiji to participate in up to 50 per cent of the proposed new service. However, before the proposal to acquire the Tarros class ships could be further developed, Island governments, either alone or in association with Australia and New Zealand, had to provide port facilities capable of handling the ships. In particular, this meant providing adequate storage space for containers, strengthening wharves where necessary and creating new berths.

The Union Company presented the concept to Pacific Forum governments at the 30 August –1 September 1972 Apia Seminar on Shipping in the South Pacific, and later reported to the New Zealand government that all countries had given a positive hearing to the proposal. In fact only Fiji had formally given a favourable response and other Island nations were slow to reply. Company management became increasingly frustrated at their inaction.[56]

Such a delay was understandable given the investigation being carried out by the South Pacific Bureau for Economic Co-operation (SPEC) into the establishment of a regional shipping line. The Tarros proposal was probably further weakened when Bill Martin of the New Zealand Seamen's Union made it clear that dual rates of pay would not be tolerated. This ruled out the possibility of significant numbers of Islanders being employed and, as such, offended Island nationalism.

> . . . the union would not accept a 'dual rate' system of seamen's wage rates—it was their policy and the policy of the Federation of Labour to increase the standard of living of the Island workers and not to lower it or alternatively to accept in principle the low rates of pay presently being paid to Island crews.[57]

The Tongan response came early in 1973. The Kingdom would not guarantee priority access to Nuku'alofa wharf and could not guarantee that Union Company container vessels would be the only such ships to use it. Moreover, Tonga was unwilling to provide any money towards the redevelopment of wharf facilities. New Zealand Foreign Affairs officials noted that this decision had to be seen in the light of Tonga's own attempts to develop a shipping company, as well as the SPEC investigation into a regional shipping line and rumours about the Union Company's possible withdrawal from the Pacific.[58]

Fiji's positive initial response was tempered by Fijian dockworkers' concerted opposition to any move towards containerisation which would reduce job opportunities. Nauru was busy with the development of its fleet and most notable in its support of the uneconomic trial visits of its conventional vessel *Cenpac Rounder* to Pacific ports. Samoa was particularly aware of its total dependence on the Union Company. Minister of Marine Tupuola Efi was keen to ensure alternative services in the short term and, while not opposed to the Union Company proposal, was more interested in subsidies for other services. At this stage Samoa was sympathetic to Nauru and Tonga's proposal of a regional shipping line.[59]

The unwillingness of Island governments to agree to the Union Company's offer left its management in a quandary. This was resolved by initiating the Tarros proposal on its own, conscious of the fact that falling southbound freight and the high capital costs associated with the new ships left the company extremely vulnerable to competition.

Karlander, the major carrier of Australian trade to Papua New Guinea and the Pacific Islands, put forward a proposal to develop a containerised Pacific service in association with Island governments, but this received little support. The concept was modified to the possibility of a joint operation of the new regional shipping line but this, too, was rejected by Forum countries.[60]

The PIPA Proposal 1970–75

By the late 1960s there had been considerable discussion on the formation of a regional shipping line, and both Tonga and Nauru had purchased their own ships. Hefty rises in freight costs in 1969–71, uncertainty over the intentions of the Union Company, and Island national and regional aspirations meant that Tonga was first able to gain support for its proposal for a regional line at the April 1971 Pacific Island Producers' Association conference in Nuku'alofa.

Tongan Minister of Finance Mahe Tupouniua spoke about the high priority placed on the formation of a regional shipping plan, and the meeting set up a working party 'to investigate fully the organisation and operation of a Regional Shipping Line based mainly on the existing facilities of the Tongan Shipping Agency so as to encourage . . . development into a fully representative regional shipping line.'[61]

The Tongan move was not surprising. Their adviser on shipping, Captain Hill-Willis, had encouraged them to unite their shipping assets into one company, optimistically predicting that the loss-making assets would make a profit that year. At the same time, he was content to have the operation investigated by a Suva-based accountancy firm.[62]

The working party set up by PIPA proposed establishing a company, to be called Seapacific Limited, based on the Tongan shipping fleet, with vessels registered in the Kingdom. There would be three Tongan directors and one each appointed by the other PIPA members. The head office was to be in Nuku'alofa and the company was to be granted limited tax exemption and priority in the use of the port. However, the project was contingent on two reviews commissioned by SPEC. A Fijian accountancy firm was contracted first to investigate the value of the assets of the Tongan Shipping Agency and then to undertake a detailed revenue projection for the next five years.[63]

As the first South Pacific Forum was held in Wellington in August 1971, before the working party had reported its findings, Forum leaders decided to await the completion of this report, as well as a United Nations-funded regional transport survey which was also in progress.[64] Regional shipping was next discussed by Forum Ministers of Transport at the shipping seminar in Apia.

Samoa's Tupuola Efi had withheld his full support from the PIPA proposal, preferring that New Zealand tackle its union movement on what appeared to be intolerance of Island-based ships operating in New Zealand ports. In the meantime he would have preferred a subsidised service to Samoa to compete with the Union Company.[65] When it became clear that a subsidy would not be forthcoming, Tupuola Efi, supported by other PIPA countries, called for a conference of Ministers of Transport and unions to be held in Apia to discuss the problems of regional shipping.

These included the fragmentation of services, the huge increases in freight rates in the previous two years, the low unit value/high bulk of Island exports, the need to replace conventional freighters with more modern ships, the slow turn-around of vessels in port and the imbalance of north- and south-bound freight. Pacific shipping was also plagued by unreasonably high pilferage, rising costs due to inflation and the lack of container facilities.[66]

None of these problems was new and there was little chance that the meeting would resolve them. New Zealand officials identified three key issues where results could be expected at the conference. The first was whether New Zealand unions would allow Island vessels to trade to and from New Zealand. The second was the likely reaction of Island leaders to the Union Company's proposal to replace its three-ship service with two Tarros class vessels. The third was the fate of the regional shipping line proposal.[67]

When Bill Martin of the New Zealand Seamen's Union made it clear that the union would protect union members' jobs on traditional routes, it was inferred that unless Islanders were members of the New Zealand union their involvement in the trade would be opposed. This was not well received by Island leaders, and the union's qualified support for the Union Company's Tarros plan removed any possibility that Island governments would take up the equity offered as part of the Union Company proposal. The reactions to these issues forced Samoa to be more positive about the Tongan proposal for a regional shipping line.

However, the Fiji accountants' report on the Tonga Shipping Agency described Captain Hill-Willis as a 'one-man band', emphasised the agency's consistent losses, saw 'no prospect of profits' and pointed out that a limited company could not continue indefinitely if it always incurred losses. The accountants recommended that any regional shipping operation should involve the expertise of one major foreign-owned shipping company.[68]

As a consequence of this, Tupuola Efi withheld his endorsement from any regional line based on the Tongan Shipping Agency and emphasised the need to include Australia and New Zealand, partly to facilitate regional trade but also to assist in overcoming the New Zealand unions' hostility:

> . . . he said that the realities of the situation—the extent of the trade with Australia and New Zealand, the attitude of the New Zealand Seamen's Union and the attitude of the New Zealand Government—dictated the need for a regional scheme which might include the Unions, the Union Company, Australia and New Zealand. It was a question of minimum risk.[69]

The PIPA and UNESCAP reports were considered at the third Forum meeting in Suva in September 1972, which established the South Pacific Bureau for Economic Co-operation (SPEC) and charged this organisation with determining the viability of a regional shipping line. SPEC acquired the services of Australian shipping adviser Dr Brian Fitzwarryne, whose report to the April 1973 Apia Forum included a framework for a possible shipping line. However, the Forum decided to integrate the Fitzwarryne report with a further SPEC paper on regional trade. When these studies were complete they were to be reviewed by officials and referred back to the Forum.

The South Pacific Bureau for Economic Co-operation (SPEC) headquarters in Suva were completed in 1976.

Fitzwarryne completed the SPEC report in early 1974. It canvassed possible ownership options ranging from joint operations with current shipping companies to a fully funded regional line. Fitzwarryne noted that the possible advantages of the latter included economies of scale, rationalised timetables, Islander employment, improved port facilities and a reinforcement of Island nationalism[70] —although he also warned of the considerable financial risk such a proposal entailed. Perhaps most important was his confirmation that any successful regional line would have trade en route to New Zealand, which would be considered cross-trading by the New Zealand unions.[71]

While it appeared that the Forum could proceed with a regional shipping line, planning for a regional airline, Air Pacific, began to fall apart as other island nations—most notably Tonga and Nauru—set up their own airlines. This development severely shook some Island governments' faith in the concept of regional co-operation. Fiji's Ratu Sir Kamisese Mara was particularly dismayed because the regional airline proposal had been based on developing the Fijian carrier.

Plans for a shipping line were still at a preliminary stage. At the March 1974 Rarotonga Forum it was decided to press on and establish the South Pacific Regional Shipping Council to set policy guidelines, but the heads of government once again favoured further studies before making any formal decision to proceed.

Australia had considerable economic and political reservations whether the establishment of a regional line would remedy the perceived problems of Pacific shipping. The Australian government requested the Australian National Line (ANL) to estimate the viability of providing a container service between Australia, Samoa, Tonga and Fiji. ANL's study showed that, even with Island provision of port facilities, the service would lose A\$3 million a year, and it was deemed inappropriate to divert aid to cover an ongoing loss.[72]

There was also unease in Australia that New Zealand was seeking commercial and diplomatic aggrandisement in the Pacific through building up its Shipping Corporation, presumably at the expense of Australian shipping interests, yet simultaneously seeking to reduce its joint service to the Cook Islands and Niue. These concerns appear most succinctly in a draft brief for the Australian delegation to the June 1975 Suva Pacific Regional Shipping Council:

> New Zealand, for political reasons, supports the idea of establishing a regional shipping line, as a means of expanding the operations of the Shipping Corporation of N.Z. and spreading the burden of the losses on maintaining services to the Cook Islands and Niue.[73]

Australian concerns seem to have been related to New Zealand's intention to have a New Zealand crew on at least one regional line vessel to placate New Zealand unionists and to a fear that this might reduce effective Island involvement.[74]

Dutch shipping expert Brian de Vlaming, who had recently retired from Nedlloyds, was engaged to co-ordinate a range of studies to investigate Pacific trade flows and the possibility of pooling current shipping resources. He established a SPEC team headed by Francis Hong Tiy and the challenge for those involved in the survey was to convert value and weight statistics into volume since an assessment of freight volumes would ascertain the viability of any new service.[75]

Studies presented to the Regional Shipping Council in Suva in June 1975 produced a schedule of development for the regional shipping project. If approved by the forthcoming Forum, it was envisaged that the line could be established by June 1976. Prior to this, the study had to demonstrate that a regional line could be commercially viable, and also determine 'the best routes for the new line, the types of ships required and cargoes to be carried.'[76] The council's recommendations were

At the Rarotonga Forum leaders decided to establish the South Pacific Regional Shipping Council, which was charged with setting regional shipping policy. From left: Ratu Sir Kamisese Mara, Prime Minister, Fiji; Senator Don Willesee, Minister of Foreign Affairs, Australia; Norman Kirk, Prime Minister, New Zealand; Hammer DeRoburt, President, Nauru; Michael Somare, Chief Minister, Papua New Guinea; Robert Rex, Leader of Government Business, Niue; Albert Henry, Premier, Cook Islands; HRH Prince Fatafehi Tu'ipelehake, Prime Minister, Tonga; Fiame Mata'afa, Prime Minister, Samoa.

accepted at the July 1975 Nuku'alofa Forum, although there was still considerable uncertainty as to the attitude of the New Zealand maritime unions.

To minimise the initial capital outlay, de Vlaming's team recommended that the participating countries operate a pooling system whereby they contributed ships on a charter basis and/or working capital. This meant that it was possible to involve crew from outside New Zealand while still maintaining a New Zealand crew on New Zealand vessels. The consultants proposed two profitable trunk routes emanating from New Zealand and Australia and visiting major islands including Tonga, Fiji and the Samoas. A third route was also brought to the attention of Forum leaders. This was from New Zealand to Papua New Guinea and the Solomons, although the study suggested that this would need development before proving profitable.

On this basis, the Regional Shipping Council recommended to the Forum that immediate steps be taken to form the shipping line. This was accepted at the Forum meeting in Nauru in July 1976.

New Zealand Prime Minister Robert Muldoon drinking kava at the opening of the SPEC headquarters.

CHAPTER TWO

Setting Up the Line

THE DE VLAMING REPORTS were important in establishing confidence in the potential of a regional line but the process of reaching agreement on the shape of the organisation was a major political challenge. Decisions had to be made about how each country could participate so that all Pacific nations would have an equitable stake in the regional carrier.

The South Pacific Forum accepted de Vlaming's suggestion of a pooling system whereby participating countries contributed vessels under charter to the line. This removed any need for capital to buy ships. It was believed that working capital contributions should be within the means of smaller Pacific Island states and profits or losses were to be apportioned to the participants according to their contributions. In the end the share capital chosen was WS$10,000 with a total capital of WS$100,000.[77] This was recognised at the time as a very sparse capital base, but officials were deluded by a naive optimism born of limited commercial expertise and bolstered by the belief that political support could make up for any commercial failings.

Although the de Vlaming studies suggested that two of the three projected routes would instantly prove profitable, they were based on some odd assumptions. One of these was that the Pacific Forum Line's entry into the market would not be opposed by other operators. Such confidence was warranted only if the new line entered into trade-sharing agreements with those already servicing the Pacific. However, even if the other companies would have accepted such a proposal, it was clear that some shareholders would not. The government of Nauru, while a PFL shareholder, was also the owner of a competing company and absolutely opposed to any shipping conference or similar reduction in competition.[78] The Australian High Commissioner relayed President DeRoburt's attitude to the High Commission in Suva.

> I was able to check out the President's thinking very quickly, as last Friday he hosted a party on the *Enna G*, which had been kept in port an additional day to permit the Nauru Local Government Council to have a party on her to celebrate the recent expenditure on her latest refit (as a container carrier) . . . He left me in no doubt that his position remains the same as in April. His point is that the present shipping lines, Columbus, Farrell, etc., do not operate as a bloc and are in competition with one another, why then should the Regional Line of the countries of the area make it easier for them to operate—should it not meet them head-on in and take business away from them?[79]

The assumption of instant profitability permitted officials to avoid the awkward question of who would provide working capital. While only the wealthier nations in the region had the means to fund the line in any significant way, this would cause problems if it was reflected in relative shareholding. Smaller countries would not want to lose influence and status because they were contributing less. Officials hoped that the equity would grow so quickly that there would be no need for significant development capital and that each state would benefit equally from the growth. Such an assumption was at odds with contemporary Pacific shipping experience, which suggested that establishing any new route was risky, expensive and likely to unleash considerable competitive forces.

It had been envisaged that the line would have a multi-layered structure. Agents and head office staff were to be responsible to a general manager who was in turn responsible to the board of directors. Up to this level the structure was to be conventional; but the reality of a line owned by ten governments was that political accountability would be superimposed on the commercial structure. As a result, the Regional Shipping Council was charged with setting general policy for the board.

The June 1975 Regional Shipping Council meeting had recommended that countries contributing ships (shipping members) should have a seat on the board of directors as of right, but that countries committing only finance should also be eligible for representation. It was intended that regional representation be as wide as possible but, recognising that too large a board could be ineffective, the shipping council favoured a board of seven.

This meeting had also decided on the name—the Pacific Forum Line (PFL)[80]—

which was significant because it expressed the unique relationship between the line and the Forum. It is one of the few modern trading companies whose origins lie in international diplomacy.

A group of officials—the South Pacific Regional Shipping Advisory Board—had been established to facilitate the establishment of the Forum Line. It was served and led by the South Pacific Bureau for Economic Co-operation. These officials did much of the spadework in co-ordinating government input. One involved in the process commented, with 1990s hindsight, that co-ordinating a government's contribution to the establishment of an operating company would now be considered impractical; whereas the notion of co-ordinating that of seven governments would be totally rejected.[81]

The Memorandum of Understanding, which was both the international agreement between the nations and the basis of the articles of association of the company, was drafted by officials. It is a long, complex document whose main points need only be summarised. The first was that a company called the Pacific Forum Line would be established under the laws of Samoa. Each contracting party was to invest WS$10,000 as part of a total capital of WS$100,000. None of the participants was to be able to sell its shares except back to other shareholders, so that control would remain with the governments. The memorandum encompassed procedures for the allocation of profits but was less clear on the signatories' responsibility for losses. Contracting parties—that is, the governments—had to give a year's notice of intention to withdraw from the line.[82]

The line's principal goal was to operate ships, whether purchased or chartered, to meet the special shipping circumstances of the region. Profits were to be allocated between the shareholders according to their shareholdings, which in 1977 were equal. The line was to be administered through the board of directors and the Regional Shipping Council, with the latter determining general policy. The role of the board was to implement general policy, enter into charters, borrow money and set commercial policy. The board was also to appoint a general manager responsible for the day-to-day operations of the company.

The memorandum and articles did not oblige member governments to use the line. They recognised that PFL would have to operate commercially in competition with other shippers and had faith that it would quickly gain market share at the expense of what were perceived as the current, inefficient operators.

The Political Context

The time taken to investigate the establishment of the Pacific Forum Line was determined by political as well as commercial considerations. In particular Australia was much less keen on the concept of a regional shipping line than New Zealand and the Island governments.

Samoa's Tupuola Efi was particularly frustrated by the delays. At the 1976 Nauru Forum meeting he put considerable pressure on New Zealand and Australia to deliver or, he suggested, other countries might be prepared to help:

> . . . there is a new urgency in the South Pacific, new challenges. The Russians want things and the Chinese want to compete with the Russians. The non-aligned countries are attempting to attract the aligned countries. At the non-aligned meeting in Colombo all Heads of Government will be present; but the Australian Head of Government was not in Nauru . . . If they did not see progress through the activities of traditional donors they will ask why other offers were being rejected.[83]

New Zealand Prime Minister Robert Muldoon was conciliatory and supported the PFL concept. Indeed, he stressed in his reply that it had bi-partisan support in New Zealand:

> . . . there seemed to be some misunderstanding of the New Zealand attitude. New Zealand was in favour of the line and he was astonished that anybody could think otherwise. The New Zealand Labour Government had moved forward in the face of considerable obstacles—the Waitangi Conference had been an important breakthrough. The real problem was the unions, who see a diminishing membership as coastal ships go off. The National Government had picked up where the Labour Government left off. It had been working closely with the unions and has enlisted the assistance of Sir Tom Skinner. . . . [Muldoon] agreed that unless the Forum took a decision now to establish the Pacific Forum Line, there may never be a regional line.[84]

Senator Cotton, the Australian representative, said that his country supported the PFL concept and would be happy to provide aid and technical know-how but would not provide capital because of the financial risk. Australia was uncomfortable with the concept of a line established without significant capital backing, in part because its shipping advisers considered that, to be competitive with the Union Company, the Pacific Forum Line would have to buy two container ships at a cost of some A$5 million each. Despite Australia's doubts, the Forum voted for the establishment of the line.

Even with that agreement, Pacific leaders grew frustrated at what appeared to be a lack of progress while new shipping companies entered the market. In 1976 Papua New Guinea established its own line and, in early 1977, Tonga entered an agreement with Danish refrigerated shipping specialist Lauritzens to bail out the Pacific Navigation Company. It was also known that Tonga was negotiating with the German-owned Columbus Line to develop further its shipping assets.[85]

Samoan concern centred around the New Zealand unions' refusal to accept cross-trading. Economic Affairs Minister Asi Eikeni pinpointed the problem when he asked:

> If a roll-on roll-off ship cannot operate on a direct route as envisaged in a marketing survey, it will have to do a circular route and this means 'cross-trading'. Will the New Zealand maritime unions allow a cross-trading vessel in the Pacific to enter a New Zealand port?[86]

In 1977 Papua New Guinea set up its own shipping corporation before the PFL was established. The Papua New Guinea Post Courier *depicted the move as putting Papua New Guinea in competition with PFL in a restricted market.*

The Union Issue

Asi Eikeni's caution was justifiable. At the Waitangi conference the maritime unions had stated that 'more permanent regional shipping arrangements which included significant Island participation would only be accepted if the situation regarding employment opportunities for New Zealand seamen was at least maintained.' Because of the smouldering *Enna G* dispute, the unions and SPEC officials had not agreed on any formal acceptance of ITF wage rates, and New Zealand union acceptance could not be expected when the employment of New Zealand seamen fell approximately 25 per cent in 1975—largely as a result of a drop in conventional cargo and a consequent restructuring of the Union Company.

Although it was more expensive to have a New Zealand crew on the Forum Line's Pacific routes, it was necessary to placate the New Zealand maritime unions. The New Zealand Secretary of Transport saw no other option. 'As the Pacific Forum Line is envisaged as taking up 25 per cent of the New Zealand/Pacific Island trade, it appears essential that New Zealand maritime employees participate in the manning of Forum Line vessels serving the trade. It is therefore necessary that the prospect of New Zealand contributing a vessel to the shipping pool be thoroughly investigated.'

Because of industrial relations sensitivity, each Forum government was instructed to consult with its own unions. The New Zealand Ministers of Labour and Transport were to inform the unions of the current situation, ascertain their attitude to cross-trading by the Forum Line, seek their co-operation in manning any vessel that New Zealand might contribute to the line, and impress upon leaders the necessity for co-operation.[87]

Union appeasement came at an additional price for the New Zealand taxpayer. Use of a New Zealand crew paid at New Zealand award wages would make the annual charter rate of the ship considerably higher than that which could be obtained on the world market. PFL's use of a New Zealand ship was out of the question unless the New Zealand government made up the difference.[88] The resultant charter subsidy was initially estimated at NZ$0.3 million a year but once operations began it ballooned to over ten times that amount. The likelihood of paying a similar subsidy to reduce the cost of any Australian vessel led to Australia's decision not to participate directly in the Forum Line.

The Choice of Ships

Despite a general recognition of the need to develop containerisation to modernise the service, the Pacific Forum Line initially ran conventional freighters for financial reasons. The charter formula minimised capital outlay and allowed the line to be established with ships already owned or chartered by Pacific governments. It was hoped that profits would soon allow the upgrade of the ships and that expensive charters of conventional vessels would be short-term.

At the Nauru Forum it was decided that New Zealand, Nauru and Samoa would initially provide vessels. In 1977 the Muldoon government was in the process of restructuring the Cook Islands service, and the *Lorena, Luhesand* and *Toa Moana*, which had all been on the Cook Islands run, were potentially available as New Zealand's contribution to the new line. Initially the *Lorena* was offered because she was not suitable for the envisaged Cook Islands–Papeete service and would soon become available. Nauru had offered the *Cenpac Rounder* but this was deemed unsuitable. The PFL board was keen on another Nauruan ship, the *Eigamoya*, a conventional freighter which at that time was operating on the Australian–central Pacific run. A newly elected Nauruan government offered the *Eigamoya* but after the re-election of Hammer DeRoburt and only shortly before she was due to be leased to PFL, the offer was withdrawn.[89] Since Samoa's offer was dependent on a West German aid proposal which took longer than expected, they could not initially provide a vessel.

As a consequence of this uncertainty, the establishment of the Forum Line did not follow schedule and the initial decisions on vessel choice had to be revised early in 1978. New Zealand officials changed their offer from the *Lorena* to the *Toa Moana*. PFL's newly appointed board of directors responded by

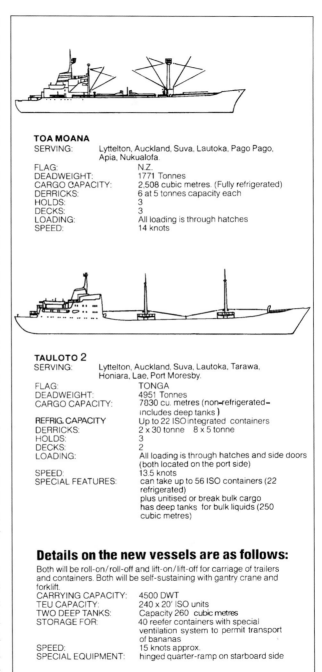

TOA MOANA
SERVING:	Lyttelton, Auckland, Suva, Lautoka, Pago Pago, Apia, Nukualofa.
FLAG:	N.Z.
DEADWEIGHT:	1771 Tonnes
CARGO CAPACITY:	2,508 cubic metres. (Fully refrigerated)
DERRICKS:	6 at 5 tonnes capacity each
HOLDS:	3
DECKS:	3
LOADING:	All loading is through hatches
SPEED:	14 knots

TAULOTO 2
SERVING:	Lyttelton, Auckland, Suva, Lautoka, Tarawa, Honiara, Lae, Port Moresby.
FLAG:	TONGA
DEADWEIGHT:	4951 Tonnes
CARGO CAPACITY:	7830 cu. metres (non-refrigerated– includes deep tanks)
REFRIG. CAPACITY	Up to 22 ISO integrated containers
DERRICKS:	2 x 30 tonne 8 x 5 tonne
HOLDS:	3
DECKS:	2
LOADING:	All loading is through hatches and side doors (both located on the port side)
SPEED:	13.5 knots
SPECIAL FEATURES:	can take up to 56 ISO containers (22 refrigerated) plus unitised or break bulk cargo has deep tanks for bulk liquids (250 cubic metres)

Details on the new vessels are as follows:

Both will be roll-on/roll-off and lift-on/lift-off for carriage of trailers and containers. Both will be self-sustaining with gantry crane and forklift.

CARRYING CAPACITY:	4500 DWT
TEU CAPACITY:	240 x 20' ISO units
TWO DEEP TANKS:	Capacity 260 cubic metres
STORAGE FOR:	40 reefer containers with special ventilation system to permit transport of bananas
SPEED:	15 knots approx.
SPECIAL EQUIPMENT:	hinged quarter-ramp on starboard side

Information from an early PFL brochure.

requesting the roll-on, roll-off *Coastal Ranger*, which was due to come off a government-subsidised Lyttelton–Wellington service.

Had New Zealand accepted the proposal the *Coastal Ranger* would have been compatible with the two vessels to be supplied by Samoa and Tonga and PFL could have begun with a fully containerised service. However, New Zealand rejected the request, mainly because the *Coastal Ranger* would require a larger charter subsidy, estimated at NZ$1.3 million compared with $1.03 million for the *Toa Moana* (both amounts well in excess of the NZ$0.3 estimated for the *Lorena*).[90]

West German Aid

The fleet which began operation in July 1978 consisted of the *Toa Moana* from New Zealand, the *Tauloto II*, which had been on charter to the Tongan Pacific Navigation Company, and the *Woolgar*, which was hastily chartered from a Norwegian company for the short term. This vessel was quickly replaced by the *Forum Niugini*, chartered from Papua New Guinea.

It was always intended that the Forum Line should operate unitised vessels. However, given the pooling arrangement, it was not clear how Pacific Island nations could afford them. Samoa and Tonga approached West Germany for help, Samoa as a former German colony with considerable cultural links which might have paved the way for financial assistance. Tonga made a formal application for a vessel for the Pacific trade, an inter-island vessel for domestic passenger cargo, an engineering workshop and/or a shipyard, and a maritime training school.

During the mid-1970s West Germany was keen to encourage shipping in the Pacific to aid development in states sympathetic to the West, to promote political security and to keep its shipyards busy. The German view was that their aid was essential. The New Zealand ambassador in Bonn informed New Zealand Foreign Affairs officials:

> If shipping is to survive in this area, and if the freight rates are maintained at an economically justifiable level, then changes in the vessel type, modes of operation and in the average tonnage per ship will be necessary in the overseas shipping sector. It would not be sufficient simply to enlarge the fleet with ships of conventional construction. Tonga needs modern tonnage which will ensure the supply of special import commodities and also be suitable for the export of Tonga's agricultural produce, especially bananas.[91]

West German officials responded positively to the Tongan and Samoan requests, combining them into a single proposal to assist internal and external shipping.[92]

Im Südpazifik bleibt Moskau vor der Tür

Australien und Neuseeland begrüßen das deutsche Engagement / Von Erhard Haubold

SYDNEY, im September
Vor zwei Jahren schickte Moskau eine hochrangige Delegation in den Südpazifik, eines der wenigen vom Wettlauf der Großmächte noch verschonten Gebiete der Welt. In Tonga und Westsamoa, kleinen, unterentwickelten, hauptsächlich von Agrarexporten le-

Seither ist es im Südpazifik wieder ruhig geworden. Die umworbenen Regierungen arbeiten lieber mit alten Freunden als mit der Sowjetunion, wie der australische Außenminister Peacock bemerkte, zumal ihr Wink verstanden worden ist: „Wenn unsere traditionel-

bleiben damit die dominierenden Kräfte. Washington denkt, so der stellvertretende Außenminister Richard Holbrooke, zwar an eine „größere und leistungsfähigere Präsenz" in den näch-

Seite 18 - Nr. 242 - Hamburger Abendblatt

Reederei hilft Samoa und Tonga:

Zwei Schwestern von Hamburg in die Südsee

Eigener Bericht

Kr. Hamburg, 16. Oktober

Wenn heute bei der Schiffswerft J. J. Sietas in Hamburg-Neuenfelde das Ro Ro-Containerschiff auf den Namen „Forum Samoa" getauft wird, geht der erste Abschnitt eines Entwicklungshilfe-Projekts zu Ende, das von der Hamburg-Süd in Zusammenarbeit mit der Bundesregierung vor zwei Jahren begonnen wurde. Die Inselreiche Westsamoa und Tonga erhalten je ein Schiff für den regionalen Verkehr zwischen Australien, Neuseeland und den pazifischen Inselstaaten.

Ziel dieser deutschen Wirtschaftshilfe ist es, eine moderne überseeische Verkehrsverbindung innerhalb dieser Region zu schaffen und damit einen Beitrag zur wirtschaftlichen Entwick-

Erwin Ludewig von der Geschäftsführung der Hamburg-Süd am Vorabend der Schiffstaufe erklärte, sollen beide Schiffe von der Pacific Forum Line eingesetzt werden. Dieses sei eine

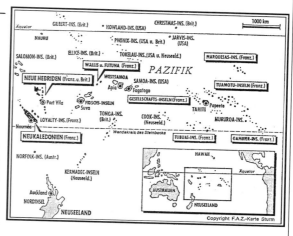

⟍ Pacific Forum von Nordeuropa

Die neuseeländische Pacific Forum Line wird in diesem Jahr zwei Abfahrten von Nordeuropa nach der Südsee durchführen. Als europäische Ladehäfen sind Hamburg, Rotterdam und Felixstowe vorgesehen. Für die Reederei entstehen gegenwärtig in Hamburg zwei kombinierte Ro/Ro- und Containerschiffe. Die Neubauten (5536 t dw und 3700 BRT) erhalten eine Kapazität für 313 TEU. Für die Aufnahme von rollendem Material wird ein Autodeck von 800 qm zur Verfügung stehen. Außerdem werden die Neubauten mit einem Bordkran von 25 t und Tieftanks ausgestattet. Die beiden Schiffe sind für den regionalen Einsatz im Südpazifik bestimmt. Die Ausreisen werden im Rahmen von Überführungsfahrten geboten.

Als erster Neubau soll die „Forum Samoa" am 16. Oktober in Hamburg an die Pacific Forum Line abgeliefert werden und in Nordeuropa für Apia, Nukualofa, Lautoka, Suva, die Cook Islands, Tuvalu, Honiara, Tarawa, Lyttelton, Napier und Auckland laden. Die Ablieferung des Schwesterschiffes „Fua Kavenga" ist für den 30. November vorgesehen.
Antwerpen von der Pegasus Shipping & Forwarding N. V., in Felixstowe von der Alltrans Express und in Rotterdam von der Pegasus Shipping & Forwarding (Rotterdam) B. V. vertreten. Letztere ist gleichzeitig Generalagent für Europa.

Kommt: König von Tonga

Tonga: Ein Schiff wird kommen...

es Hamburg — Ein farbenfroher, exotischer Staatsbesuch steht den Hamburgern im Herbst ins Haus: Taufa'ahau Topau IV. König Nuku'Alofa von Tonga (Inselgruppe in der Südsee, östlich der Fidschi-Inseln) kommt auf Besuch.
Der König wird auf der Sietas-Werft in Neuenfelde das erste Frachtschiff für Tonga übernehmen.
Ebenso wie die benachbarte Insel Samoa, deren er-

stes Schiff gerade bei Sietas im Bau ist, legt sich auch Tonga mit deutscher Hilfe ein Frachtschiff zu. Samoa war vor dem ersten Weltkrieg einmal deutsche Kolonie, fühlt sich heute den Deutschen sehr verbunden —auch wirtschaftlich.
Die beiden typgleichen Schiffe werden mit Entwicklungshilfe der Bundesregierung gebaut. Die Reederei Hamburg-Süd berät Samoa und Tonga.

The West German aid programme provided 'soft' loans enabling Samoa and Tonga to purchase the Forum Samoa *and* Fua Kavenga. *German newspapers reported the progress of the shipping project, with one commenting on how it would help to keep Moscow out of the region.*

The West German government's agent was Hamburg Süd, owners of the Columbus Line which had operated in the Pacific since 1960. Negotiations, which continued throughout 1977, were complicated since Tonga had entered into a joint venture with Lauritzens in a bid to revive the ailing fortunes of its own Pacific Navigation Company. The agreement included a clause preventing Tonga from developing further shipping lines with other companies.[93] This delayed negotiations until late 1977 when a deal was negotiated which permitted Tongan involvement in the Pacific Forum Line and continued Lauritzen's participation in the Pacific Navigation Company.

As a result, West German shipyards were to construct a 4000-tonne roll-on, roll-off, load-on load-off container vessel under a 'soft' loan; they would help with the management of inter-island ferry services; they would develop a workshop in association with New Zealand, and also establish a maritime training school similar to that established by the Columbus Line in the Gilbert and Ellice Islands.

A 4000-tonne roll-on, roll-off vessel, representing an investment of approximately A$5 million, was to become the largest shipping asset owned by Tonga. The Shipping Corporation of Polynesia was established to administer the ship and negotiate her lease to the Pacific Forum Line. Equity in the corporation was split 60 per cent Tonga and 40 per cent Columbus, although it was recognised that Columbus equity would decline over time. It was envisaged that the vessel would be ready for use in late 1979 or early 1980—too late for the Forum Line's commencement of operations.

The Tongan aid project was matched by a similar arrangement with Samoa. This was to include an identical roll-on, roll-off vessel; Samoa Shipping Services Ltd was to be set up similarly to the Shipping Corporation of Polynesia; there was to be a training school; and Hamburg Süd would assist with the management of government shipping assets, including the Savaii ferry service.[94]

Hamburg Süd's motivation appeared to be three-fold. First, the company would gain increased access to Pacific shipping. The Columbus Line had entered the Pacific in 1960–61[95] and was expanding its operations. It had initiated container shipping to New Zealand[96] and more than once incurred the wrath of Australasian unions with its use of 'foreign crews'—most notably the Gilbert and Ellice Islanders from its training school at Tarawa. Secondly, the company's actions assisted its relationship with the West German government, which was concerned about a possible increase in Soviet or Chinese influence in the Pacific. Thirdly, Hamburg Süd was also in a handy position to develop alternative shipping if PFL failed.

The 1977 Shipping Survey

In December 1977 a New Zealand working party reporting on a survey of shipping services in New Zealand and the South Pacific[97] found that Pacific shipping was still suffering from competitive pressures partly caused by a trend towards containerisation. The Union Company's container vessel *Union South Pacific* had been replaced in 1977 by the larger but older roll-on, roll-off *Marama*. Growth of exports from New Zealand to the Islands continued, yet the decline in Island exports seemed inexorable. Operations from New Zealand were very expensive, while alternative Island services were restricted to direct trade between New Zealand and the shipper's original country. At the same time not all Pacific routes had an adequate service.

Fiji's central geographical position and relatively diverse economy meant that its major ports, Suva and Lautoka, were regularly visited by the *Marama*, by Reef Shipping's non-refrigerated conventional freighter *La Bonita* and by the Pacific Shipping Line's *Tui Cakau*. Fiji was also served by several major conference lines as part of wider trade to Europe and the United States.

In late 1977 shipping services to Tonga included the *Marama*, a subsidised service operated by the Shipping Corporation of New Zealand using the *Toa Moana*, the Pacific Navigation Company's *Ha'amotaha* and three small conventional freighters operated by the Warner Pacific Line—the *Aidan*, *Frysna* and *Kemphaan*. However, the number of vessels calling at Tonga at this time disguised the impermanence of the arrangements. The *Toa Moana* service was temporary, the Tongan vessel was losing money, and the long-term commitment of the Union Company and Warner Pacific was questionable.

Samoan shipping was probably in the most precarious position among the major Island states. The Union Company provided the fortnightly *Marama* service. The *Toa Moana* called every four weeks as did the *Ha'amotaha*. There was also a visit approximately every four weeks by one of the Warner Pacific ships. However, Samoans felt particularly vulnerable because of what they rightly perceived as the uncertain future of the Union Company's operation.

A direct New Zealand–Papua New Guinea–Solomons service was provided only by Sofrana Unilines—a French company—with its conventional vessel *Capitaine Kermadec*. The China Navigation Company, Farrell Line and Sofrana Far East Line erratically served this route as part of their northern trade but, in general, freight space north was tight and there was a definite shortage of reefer (refrigerated) space. Officials noted that New Zealand missed out on export opportunities to Papua New Guinea as a consequence of inadequate shipping.

Regular services from New Zealand to New Caledonia and the New Hebrides (Vanuatu) were provided by Sofrana Unilines while irregular and infrequent calls were made by the China Navigation Company, Polish Ocean Line and Sofrana Far

East Line. In late 1977 there was no direct shipping route from New Zealand to Micronesia.

Since 1974 the Shipping Corporation had provided a service between New Zealand and the Cook Islands on two vessels chartered by the corporation and sub-chartered to the Ministry of Foreign Affairs. There had been several changes of vessel on the route and by late 1977 it was being served by the sister container vessels *Tiare Moana* and *Fetu Moana*. With the departure of the *Luhesand* from the Tahiti trade it was envisaged that the Cook Islands route would be extended to include Papeete. The motive was purely commercial: to recoup some of the losses incurred on the services. New Zealand Foreign Affairs officials were hoping that the 1977 deficit of NZ$3 million would be cut to NZ$2 million.

The overall conclusions of the New Zealand survey were that vessels tended to arrive together at Suva, Apia and Nuku'alofa, much to the frustration of exporters, and banana shippers in particular; that there was a problem over the introduction of containerisation because bananas had not, at that time, been successfully carried in containers; and that there had been a shortage of space for New Zealand exports to Fiji, although the newly established *Marama* service was expected to alleviate this. Traditional trades direct from the South Island of New Zealand to the Islands had ceased and South Island exporters were considerably disadvantaged. Finally, it was noted that the region as a whole, while not growing quickly, was one of New Zealand's top ten export destinations.

Setting Up the Company

By 20 July 1978 the first seven countries had signed the Memorandum of Understanding. This was a sufficient show of support for the establishment of the new shipping line. Australia and Niue had decided to stay out but ultimately the other Forum states joined, including Tuvalu, Kiribati, and the Solomons on gaining independence.[98] In April 1977 a provisional board had met because PFL was not at that stage formally incorporated under Samoan law. On 26 July 1977 the permanent board of directors was established with the authority of the Regional Shipping Council, consequent upon the presentation of letters of appointment. The Pacific Forum Line Ltd was registered as a private company on 7 July 1977.[99] The first directors were:

N. Slade (Chairman)	Samoa
Captain J. L. Harrison	Fiji
T. Tufui	Tonga
E. Tsitsi (Vice-Chairman)	Nauru
J. H. Bowering	Papua New Guinea
R. Shea	New Zealand
R. C. Chapman	Cook Islands[100]

Only J. H. Bowering, Captain Harrison and Ray Shea had shipping backgrounds. As assistant general manager of the Shipping Corporation of New Zealand, Shea was heavily involved with the provision of the New Zealand ship for the venture. Ordinarily his dual involvement in the leasing of this vessel would have been seen as a conflict of interest, but the charter was a 'soft' one in which New Zealand's— although theoretically not the Shipping Corporation's—commercial interests were sacrificed to ensure that a New Zealand ship could participate in the service.

New Zealand Minister of Transport Colin McLachlan was one of seven to sign the Memorandum of Understanding. Beside him is SPEC director Mahe Tupouniua.

Dewsnap's Challenge

At its second meeting in Apia on 18 October 1977, the board appointed Gordon Dewsnap as general manager. Originally from England, Dewsnap came to New Zealand in 1974 to supervise the construction of roll-on, roll-off terminals for the Union Company. After this he was made regional manager of the company in Wellington before joining PFL in December 1977.[101]

Dewsnap was constrained by the political circumstances of the establishment of the Forum Line. He was obliged to run an operation using chartered vessels when he really had no choice but to accept ships from Forum countries. His head office was in Apia, despite the fact that (as the Forum countries recognised) this was a difficult location from which to keep in touch with the rest of the south-west Pacific. As well as lacking high quality telecommunication, Apia was on the wrong side of the International Date Line and, as such, was in contact with Australasia on only four business days a week.

The general trade routes had been determined earlier by consultants, while the complexities of the industrial situation regarding New Zealand seamen and the accord between Australia and New Zealand maritime unions over trans-Tasman shipping also limited Dewsnap's freedom. He appeared to include the commercial objectives of the line under the wider political agenda of the Forum in arguing that profitability was unlikely.[102] There was a genuine, though uneven, political will among Forum members to support the new shipping line. While Samoa provided a five-year tax moratorium, other member states shied away from market support that might have contravened the General Agreement on Tariffs and Trade.[103]

Operations commenced in May 1978 on what were considered the three most profitable routes. These were the focus of an article in the *New Zealand Herald*:

In mid-1977 PFL's board advertised internationally for a general manager.

> The South Pacific Forum Line plans three new services in the south-west Pacific. Service 'A' will link New Zealand with Fiji, the two Samoas and Tonga. Service 'B' goes to Fiji, the Gilbert Islands, the Solomon Islands and Papua New Guinea, while Service 'C' links Melbourne with Sydney, Fiji, the two Samoas and Tonga.
> Service manager Captain G. R. Dewsnap said services would first be operated by fairly conventional ships carrying a mixture of unit loads, break-bulk and some containers . . . Early in 1979 new multi-purpose ships will be phased into service and services 'A' and 'C' will be combined to produce a boomerang run from Australia to the Pacific Islands, New Zealand and back to the Pacific Islands and Australia.[104]

In his media release Dewsnap was blunt about the poor timing of the line's establishment, believing that 'the middle of a recession (was) absolutely the wrong time to start a shipping company. However, after four years of planning it was impossible to wait any longer.'[105]

Cargo liftings failed to meet expectations and were often dramatically below those forecast. PFL's conventional vessels were not as suitable as had been hoped, in part because the Union Company's *Marama* had created a demand for containerised shipping but mainly because the conventional vessels had slow turn-around times at Australasian ports, which vastly increased costs. It was often quicker to discharge and load similar-sized cargoes at Island ports, despite the fact that many lacked a basic infrastructure. New Zealand's High Commissioner to Tonga wryly pointed this out in August 1978 when responding to the Columbus Line's negative assessment of facilities at Nuku'alofa:

> It was revealing to read that the Tongans must improve their cargo-handling methods. No doubt their general demeanour on the wharf needs to be looked at (people actually seem happy in their work) but the Tongans do not need to learn anything from us. We do not have the figures but they were quoted to us recently to show that working with the same cargo and inferior gear, the Tongans (and probably the Samoans) turn ships around at twice the speed we can manage. Perhaps Columbus should redirect their efforts to Auckland and Wellington.[106]

In order to contain costs and allow the Forum Line to survive until the arrival of the West German container vessels—which were anticipated in late 1978 but launched a year later[107]—PFL looked to shareholders to provide financial assistance.

Because of the political difficulties associated with approaching government shareholders, management had to act cautiously, cognisant of each state's ability to pay. In practice it meant returning frequently to New Zealand, which often obliged with a further extension of overdraft facilities. Such a strategy was inevitable because there was no working capital as there would have been in a conventional company. In the meantime the social objectives which had been important in the initial schedules had to be down-played and the number of port calls reduced.[108]

The First Five Months

After five months of operation it was clear that the initial revenue projections and assumptions about trading opportunities were grossly optimistic. The line had faced customer resistance to its conventional vessels and, as was almost inevitable, a price war had broken out when it attempted to gain market share.[109] Gordon Dewsnap and chairman Neroni Slade visited all the participating countries and Australia in November 1978 to address the urgent need for operating funds. Dewsnap estimated that the line would lose WS$800,000 to the end of December 1978, with a further loss of WS$500,000 in 1979, before the arrival of the West German roll-on, roll-off vessels. He admitted that the line had been set up with insufficient capital and noted that he now sought not only money to survive but also a re-examination of the line's capital needs.

Foundation staff outside PFL's head office, Apia, in 1978. Francis Hong Tiy is on the left and Gordon Dewsnap fifth from the left.

However, there were some positive aspects to these first months of operation. PFL had established a head office in Apia and all had gone relatively smoothly given that it was an ambitious project attempted within considerable political and financial constraints. Although finance manager Peter Goerman had resigned and been replaced by Colin Small, there was a growing and stable head office staff[110] backed up by a comprehensive system of agencies in other ports. There were new services to the Gilbert and Ellice Islands and the Solomons, and PFL had re-established the link between New Zealand's South Island and the Pacific, which the Union Company had abandoned some years previously.[111]

In that initial five months PFL earned its first WS$1 million in revenue and wrested its cargo almost exclusively from competitors, albeit at some cost. The schedule was such that a considerable number of stops were developmental rather than economic. Dewsnap reported: 'On (the) first voyage *Tauloto II* had carried 200 tonnes of cargo to the Gilberts—a very expensive call. This increased to 400 tonnes on the second call and PFL now had 600 tonnes of bookings for the third voyage.'[112] It was clear that some routes would be more profitable than others. On the first two New Zealand–Papua New Guinea voyages most of the revenue had been raised on the New Zealand–Fiji sector of the run. This route had been placed under considerable pressure with the establishment of the Papua New Guinea National Shipping Line, which had inaugurated a service very similar to PFL's. While PFL did not serve Tuvalu, it had arranged for trans-shipment from Fiji, whereas in the past freight from New Zealand had been transshipped at enormous cost via Australia.

The conventional vessel Tauloto II *at Apia.*

The front cover of PFL's first brochure shows the now familiar company logo. Designed by Aucklander Clive Gower, it depicts the line's acronym on a yellow background chosen to symbolise the warm glow of the Pacific sun.

The Forum Line's entry into the market had a noticeable impact on other Pacific shipping operators whose marketing became aggressive. In commercial terms, PFL had to pay the costs of entry into the market, a factor which had been virtually ignored in the political interpretations of the de Vlaming reports.

There were also operational problems with ships spending too long in port as the result of high maintenance requirements. The most disappointing had been the *Tauloto II*, which Dewsnap intended to replace early in 1979. The *Woolgar*, which sailed the Melbourne–Sydney–Lautoka–Suva–Apia–Pago Pago–Nuku'alofa routes, was constantly losing money, essentially because she could not handle enough containers. Her capacity was further restricted when limited break-bulk freight was carried because she became too unstable to carry double container layers. As with the *Tauloto II*, it had been decided to replace her when the six-month initial charter came to an end in January 1979. The *Woolgar* was temporarily replaced by the *Moresby Chief* (Papua New Guinea) and then in August 1979 by the *Forum Niugini* (Papua New Guinea),[113] which was leased for twelve months.

The situation was somewhat different with the *Toa Moana*. Although full on leaving New Zealand, she was consistently returning losses which were the combined effect of having too little capacity for the northbound trade and too little southbound trade for her capacity.[114]

At the Niue Forum meeting of 15–22 September 1978, PFL outlined its requirements for additional funding of some WS$1 million in order to keep operating until the end of 1979. Dewsnap also spelled out the implications of letting PFL collapse and in particular what financial liability could entail for some of the smaller shareholders.[115] By November 1978 PFL estimated it needed WS$670,000

The Woolgar *at Lyttelton in 1973.*

to survive the year until the new roll-on, roll-off vessels became available. This money was provided largely by New Zealand. However, on 31 January 1979 there was an urgent request for WS$238,000 to meet current debt, which would still leave the Shipping Corporation of New Zealand unpaid on the lease of the *Toa Moana*. New Zealand was asked to provide a further NZ$957,000 to keep the line afloat until the end of February 1979. It was clear that, to survive, PFL would need to be restructured and receive a considerable capital injection.[116]

The Forum called a special meeting of the Regional Shipping Council at which New Zealand's representative, Colin McLachlan, was charged with determining the degree of members' support for the Forum Line. All except Australia supported its continuation, although Fiji showed some ambivalence. It was nevertheless agreed that a concerted effort should be made to place PFL on a commercial footing. The greatest support came from the smaller states, particularly the Gilberts and Tuvalu, although it was recognised that services to these small islands contributed disproportionately to the losses.[117]

It was hoped that this meeting would provide the extra WS$1 million needed to maintain operations until the end of 1979 and that participants would accept a framework whereby the Islands, Australia and New Zealand each accepted a third of the losses. This was not to be. The Australian commitment of NZ$435,000, coupled with their previous grant of NZ$89,000, fell far short of the one-third amount and Australia resisted any further financial contributions. New Zealand's new contribution of NZ$520,000 on top of the overdraft guarantee of NZ$650,000 was larger than any other.

The Islands together contributed a considerable amount including Samoa (NZ$266,000), Nauru (NZ$ 226,000), and Papua New Guinea (NZ$174,000). Nevertheless, committed contributions fell short of the target by NZ$590,000 and it was clear that PFL's finances would have to be revisited in the near future. The council also decided to engage independent consultant Peter Carr to survey all aspects of PFL's operation for consideration at its next meeting at Mount Hagen in Papua New Guinea.[118]

Carr's plan, 'A Future for Pacific Forum Line', was duly prepared, although in the interim PFL lost more than had been anticipated and only continued in operation thanks to a New Zealand government grant of NZ$400,000. Losses were projected to continue for the next eighteen months whether the report was implemented or not.

The Carr report was controversial and proposed remedies at odds with political reality. It recommended that the Forum Line be wound up and a commission appointed to place more experienced shipping people at the helm of a non-commercial organisation in order to attract international aid money. The shareholders, and New Zealand in particular, objected to the idea of dissolution although it was agreed that a body was needed which could approach the international community for funds. Instead a Regional Shipping Fund was set up based at SPEC headquarters in Suva. Carr's report recommended a review of management, particularly given Captain Dewsnap's stated intention of resigning in March 1980. This was subsequently acted upon.

The other major problem was the location of the head office—Apia's communication difficulties, its distance from the main revenue source (freight out of Auckland), its inability to attract high quality staff and the cost and difficulty of convening board meetings there. It was clear, however, that Samoa would find unacceptable any suggestion that the office be moved.

The report also suggested a route structure which would provide a feeder service to Tonga and Samoa using the *Forum Niugini*. This implied that the new roll-on, roll-off vessels would never trade to their countries of ownership. New Zealand felt that, even if commercially sensible, this was politically untenable. An alternative was to replace the New Zealand vessel with a roll-on, roll-off vessel on a New Zealand–Papua New Guinea run. Peter Carr also suggested that PFL develop a better relationship with other shipping companies and not be so ready to cut rates in response to competitive pressure.[119]

Some Australian officials had considerable reservations about the Carr report, which they viewed as outdated and over-optimistic.[120] They were convinced that PFL was badly managed and were generally more scathing about its prospects than their political masters. Prime Minister Malcolm Fraser had made a short-term public commitment to the line and this implied the provision of some financial assistance at the Mount Hagen meeting. Finance and Australian International Development Aid Bureau (AIDAB) officials opposed such assistance as they increasingly viewed PFL as New Zealand's problem. This was highlighted in July 1979 by the Australian High Commissioner in Wellington:

In the current debate on the future of PFL, it is worth noting that New Zealand's commitment to the Line is dictated first and foremost by necessity and self-interest. We believe it cannot do other than support the Line to the last gasp. If the New Zealand Government tried to disengage itself from PFL, New Zealand's union(s) would first 'black' the PFL and then other ships engaged in the Pacific Trade (with the exception of the two New Zealand Shipping Corporation vessels— whose NZ crews would probably go out on strike in sympathy).[121]

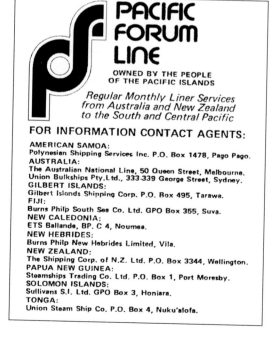

The Mount Hagen Meeting

The outcome of the Mount Hagen Regional Shipping Council meeting was mixed. On the one hand there was an agreement to fund the Forum Line until the end of 1980, with a New Zealand contribution of US$1,250,000, an Australian contribution of US$565,000 and a combined Island input of US$440,000. However, as with former pledges, obtaining the promised funds proved difficult and the financial situation remained desperate. Samoa and Tonga undertook to consider lowering charter rates on the new roll-on, roll-off vessels well below West German recommendations and New Zealand agreed to provide a RORO vessel to begin service at about the same time as the West German ships. The New Zealand vessel would be chartered by the Shipping Corporation of New Zealand in the same way as the *Toa Moana*, with the Ministry of Foreign Affairs subsidising its operation. It was also agreed to offer the *Toa Moana* to the Forum Line at a nil charter fee in the interim.[122]

The meeting was widely reported in the media, where New Zealand commentators questioned the amount of money being pumped into the line by New Zealand. For the first time it was obvious to the New Zealand and Pacific Islands public that only New Zealand largesse had saved PFL.[123] Also at this meeting, Captain Dewsnap's intention to resign in March 1980 was officially announced.

Gordon Dewsnap's achievement in establishing the line was considerable. He had intended to stay in Samoa but his relationship with the Samoan government had deteriorated. After clashing with Prime Minister Tupuola Efi over the schedules and the establishment of the accounting office in New Zealand,[124] he eventually decided to resign rather than inflame an already tense situation.

The Mount Hagen meeting established the SPEC fund for regional shipping which could channel international as well as New Zealand aid into PFL. There were minor changes to the board, which effectively removed the original distinction between shipping and non-shipping members, and it was agreed that the council should revamp the Forum Line's management. For the first time the problems associated with the head office location were addressed—although with no resolution.[125] In turn the council decided to engage a different set of consultants, Touche Ross, to examine commercial restructuring to make the line profitable.

Most Forum states were looking forward to PFL's roll-on, roll-off service. However, they were unnerved when it became clear that the Union Company would withdraw its vessel once the West German-built vessels were introduced. This particularly frustrated Tupuola Efi, who had consistently striven for a greater choice of shipping services to his country. Fate and economics ensured Samoa's continued reliance on one operator—albeit one owned by the region's governments.[126]

However, when it became clear that the *Forum Samoa* was scheduled to visit Samoa only on an eight-weekly basis a crisis developed between the Samoan Prime Minister and PFL management.

Shipping Corporation of New Zealand acted as agent for the Solomons and Papua New Guinea. The Shipping Corporation became PFL's sole Auckland agent and UMS were given notice that PFL intended to set up its own agency in Samoa, where UMS had been the agents since 1979.

The Apia PFL agency commenced operations on 1 May 1982 and not only handled its own freight but increasingly sought general agencies for other companies.[166] The Wellington administration office was moved to Auckland in December 1981 to become the major centre of operations.[167]

Fiji's commitment to seeking European Community funds succeeded. Since aid was not available to fund past operating losses and could only be used to fund development, Fiji applied for extra finance to allow PFL to build sufficient containers to reduce its heavy reliance on hiring them.

A 1981 Australian grant of A$1.5 million had been used to purchase 140 containers which, it was anticipated, would reduce PFL lease costs by some NZ$500,000 by the end of 1983. However, it was the prospect of a European Investment Bank loan of US$6 million which held out real hope of revitalising PFL. The South Pacific Bureau for Economic Co-operation had also applied for a US$1 million Lomé grant for further containers. Nevertheless, PFL had to continue trading and appear potentially viable before such monies could be disbursed.[168]

In April 1982 European Investment Bank officials visited Auckland to carry out a thorough study of the Forum Line. They then offered a loan which was accepted by Forum leaders at the South Pacific Forum in August 1982 and approved by EIB directors the following October.[169]

This loan was based on an agreed ratio between the Forum Line's assets and liabilities which laid down that each shareholder had to contribute on time and according to the schedules. If, for any reason, PFL did not perform according to projections, the shortfall would have to be made up. Moreover, Australian contributions from bilateral aid remained subject to the proviso that Island states should identify what was to be cut from their individual allocations. The result was that, despite these commitments, the New Zealand overdraft remained extremely important to PFL's survival during 1982–83 and it was hoped that the European Community would continue its support even though, at times, the asset ratios were breached.

Despite ongoing losses, there was optimism at the Rotorua Forum. In addition to the European Investment Bank's US$6 million, a further US$12.6 million was to be provided by shareholders to capitalise the line. New Zealand committed US$6.3 million, Australia US$2.3 million, while the seven island ACP shareholders contributed US$4 million.[170]

However, the Forum Line's dependence on its overdraft was reinforced when its 1982–83 losses were US$7 million greater than those anticipated even by the EIB. This was largely ascribed to the recession which hit the Australasian economies.

The immediate impact on PFL was that the EIB could not pay over loan monies until the asset ratios had returned to those set out in the loan. While New Zealand agreed to cover US$3.5 million of the money needed,[171] it was difficult to see where the remaining half might come from.[172] The newly elected Australian Labour government had no intention of altering the previous administration's policy and, if anything, was committed to a more rigid interpretation of the Rotorua agreement.[173] The EIB made it clear that it had no choice but to delay disbursements until the ratios were at an appropriate level. This new challenge was not easily met and, while the wrangling over debt liability kept the politicians busy, PFL management grappled with trying to improve returns.

The Brisbane Service

In the latter part of 1981 it was decided that, to increase earnings, *Forum New Zealand* would enter the trans-Tasman trade from Brisbane. This departed somewhat from the original concept of the line as a service provider to the Pacific Islands. After negotiations with the Australian National Line, the Shipping Corporation of New Zealand and the Union Company, a joint charter arrangement was arranged with the Union Company. Although the Union Company withdrew from the agreement within a year, PFL regularly carried between 35 and 40 containers from Brisbane by the end of 1982. This was acceptable to Australasian unions because the vessel had a New Zealand crew. In July 1982 it was decided to attempt a service from New Zealand to Brisbane via Papua New Guinea. This also proved successful and grew to match the reciprocal trade.[174] PFL later introduced a service to Noumea.

These changes were vital in the attempt to turn the Forum Line around but they could not make up for the considerable down-turn in trade suffered from September 1982 until late 1983. Worst hit was the service to Papua New Guinea where cargo fell by 49 per cent. At the same time PFL faced predatory pricing from two competitors—the Polish Ocean and Diamond Lines—both of whom lasted only a short time. Traditional competitors such as Karlander also cut rates to maintain market share. Harry Julian and Robert Muldoon knew that without a considerable improvement in the terms of trade, PFL would not survive.

Robert Muldoon showed his concern when he took the unusual step of speaking out publicly against Diamond's operation while on a visit to Papua New Guinea in February 1983. Diamond, with Japanese-owned ships flying the Panamanian flag of convenience and crewed by Koreans, had entered the New Zealand–Papua New Guinea trade in September 1982. Its break-bulk ships successfully targeted bulk cargoes, particularly the valuable cement trade, for which PFL's container vessels were ill-equipped.

The matter had strategic as well as financial implications for PFL because Papua New Guinea had consistently asked the line to provide service with a break-bulk vessel. New Zealand and Papua New Guinean unions had objected to cross-trading by Diamond and negotiated to have the vessels crewed by their respective nationals. In a radio interview, Robert Muldoon firmly stated that there was not enough trade for three operators. He was critical of Diamond's price cutting and predicted that the Japanese-owned service would not survive. The *National Business Review* in New Zealand observed that if that scenario proved accurate, then exporters to Papua New Guinea could expect considerable increases in freight charges.[175]

Shareholder support could sustain PFL for a brief period, but longer-term returns had to improve. By the time of the 1983 Canberra Forum there was a definite limit to what could be achieved by further restructuring of the line. Harry Julian despaired that he was spending 60 to 70 per cent of his time on PFL business despite involvement in four other operations, and stated that he was hard-pressed to produce extra initiatives, such as introducing short-term profit-making voyages to Singapore and Melbourne, without destroying PFL's reputation for regularity.[176]

Robert Muldoon smiles as his Australian counterpart Bob Hawke introduces him to Foreign Affairs Minister Bill Hayden. By the end of the Canberra Forum the relationship was less cordial.

The 1983 Canberra South Pacific Forum

A second and more bitter public clash between Australia and New Zealand leaders occurred at the fourteenth South Pacific Forum at Canberra. The central issue was Australia's unwillingness to contribute an extra US$3.5 million to rescue PFL.

Robert Muldoon described New Zealand as a Pacific supporter and suggested that Australian officials were not. He was scathing about the Australian refusal to join the bail-out and claimed that PFL was doomed without Australian support. When asked whether it would be Australia's fault if PFL went under, he replied:

> Well, it is not a question of whether I hold Australia responsible. I think the facts speak for themselves. But if the Pacific Forum Line collapses it will be the end of the biggest thing that the Forum has done in the fourteen years of its history and that will be a very, very great pity. Where the responsibility lies is for others to say.

Nevile Lodge of Wellington's Evening Post *carried Muldoon's dead duck analogy one step further.*

Muldoon did, however, isolate Australian officials and accuse them of a lack of sympathy for Pacific aspirations. He went on to say that PFL was designed to provide the Pacific with regular shipping that it had never had in the past. Asked if he was saying that Australian bureaucrats were 'Pacific ignorant', he retorted, 'That would not be too strong a statement. Pacific ignorant would be a very, very fair comment.'[177]

Angered by Muldoon's broadside, Australian Foreign Affairs Minister Bill Hayden met journalists soon afterwards. He argued that it had been a prudent decision by the Fraser government not to become a PFL shareholder because rigorous analysis showed that the Forum Line could not be economically viable. He also noted that PFL operated in a region where there was a gross excess of shipping tonnage. Hayden emphasised that this was Australia's 'very sober assessment of the situation', and that his country was not embarrassed by turning down the request.[178]

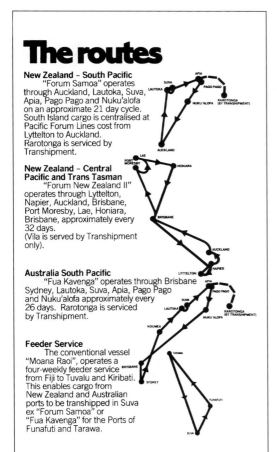

Reports in the Islands of the conflict at the Forum tended to favour New Zealand's position.

The Forum Line Survives

This public altercation masked the fact that Australia had decided to provide no further financial assistance other than aid-committed funds. Aware of the Forum Line's trading position and the likelihood that it would collapse under its debt, it was leaving New Zealand to sustain the line in the hope of an upturn in trade.

Fortunately this occurred and, assisted by an increase in the New Zealand-guaranteed overdraft to over NZ$12 million, PFL continued to trade and managed almost always to maintain its asset ratios. Crucial to this was the European Community decision to fund a loan to Papua New Guinea to increase PFL capital.[179] By February 1984 the improvement in trade figures had reduced the overdraft to NZ$6.15 million.[180]

The Pacific Forum Line's board of directors in 1983. Back row: George Fulcher (General Manager), G. Zurenouc (Director Papua New Guinea), C. I. Small (Financial Controller and Secretary); Seated: T. H. Tufui (Director Tonga), H. L. Julian (Chairman), H. Retzlaff (Director Samoa).

Continued cost-cutting strained Forum diplomatic relations. From 1 January 1984, the board cut the *Fua Kavenga* and *Forum Samoa* charter rates from US$5180[181] to US$3000 per day. The New Zealand vessel's charter was reduced to US$4000 per day—a higher rate because it was larger and faster than the two Island container ships.

This move reflected management's intention to run the line on a commercial basis—an approach accepted by shareholders. The new rates could be commercially justified in a depressed market but they dealt a considerable blow to the Tongan, Samoan and West German governments. The reaction was immediate and angry, with the owners arguing that the new rate did not even cover their expenses. There was considerable evidence to support this view and it was probably only the line's dire financial position which stopped the shipowners from unilaterally withdrawing their vessels.[182] Samoan representatives sent to West Germany to examine the possibility of a moratorium on repayments on their vessel[183] negotiated a two-year postponement on the repayment of principal only.[184]

Competition on the main Pacific routes eased with the collapse of the Diamond Line in late 1983 and withdrawal of the Polish Line in April 1984.[185] George Fulcher was then able to predict that, given the current volume of trade, the Forum Line would break even in 1985.[186] He emphasised that the real problem had been under-capitalisation, which had been remedied by the injection of nearly US$18 million in the previous twelve months.

The Pacific Forum Line entered its seventh operational year with an unenviable record of losses but with the real prospect of a sustainable profit.

The Forum New Zealand.

PFL's destinations in 1986–87.

Pacific Forum Line

We run the Pacific, regularly.

Preceding page:
The *Forum Samoa* at Lyttelton
The *Forum Tokelau* at Tokelau

This page:
The *Forum Samoa* departing Auckland
and at Bledisloe Wharf, Auckland

The *Forum Papua New Guinea* departing Auckland

The *Forum Samoa* at Queens Wharf, Auckland

Pacific Forum Line
We run the Pacific, regularly

The *Fua Kavenga* at Pago Pago, American Samoa

The *Forum Papua New Guinea* at Lae, Papua New Guinea

CHAPTER FOUR

Profitability at Last

THE PACIFIC FORUM LINE had managed to stave off financial collapse in the period after the Canberra Forum with considerable assistance from Pacific Island states and European Community aid, including the European Investment Bank loan and Lomé funds. Significant improvements in the line's earnings meant that the additional US$7 million requirement announced at Canberra was revised to US$4.8 million. While the upturn in trade and shareholder government contributions did not quite meet the EIB loan conditions, the Island nations and the South Pacific Bureau for Economic Co-operation convinced the bank that the flow-on would allow the line to break even in 1985–86.

Touche Ross independently assessed the proposals, pronounced them sound, and the loans proceeded.[187] True to predictions, PFL attained profitability after previous losses had been written off and the line had been capitalised. This was a remarkable achievement and one that augured well for the future. It was also timely, since continuing Australian opposition to further funding and the pro-market orientation of the newly elected New Zealand Labour government meant that the likelihood of Australian and New Zealand taxpayer support had diminished.

However, not all concessional funds had been exhausted. As part of a second Lomé funding round, the European Community had agreed to make available up to US$3.5 million for a suitable project. The request for funds was resubmitted in July 1984 and US$2.4 million was allocated for further container purchases.

PFL's first profit was a positive result of protracted restructuring, owing much to the Touche Ross recommendations, management changes and the capitalisation required by the European Investment Bank.

The line had also been fortunate that, by the mid-1980s, competition had eased on the most profitable routes. The Pacific Line was now the only major competitor operating three-weekly services in tandem with PFL on the New Zealand–Fiji run. It was hoped that there might be a move towards synchronised twelve-day sailings, although this seems to have reflected the enthusiasm of trade officials rather than market realities.[188] Competition had also declined on the New Zealand–Papua New Guinea run with the collapse of Diamond, although it remained intense in trade out of Australia.

A New Zealand Labour Government

The election of the Lange government in New Zealand had considerable implications for PFL. The most immediate was the removal of chairman Harry Julian. His close association with Robert Muldoon and clashes with the third Labour government over the Cook Islands service meant that, despite his important contribution to PFL's greatly improved performance, he was asked to resign.

He did so but upset protocol by communicating his resignation to the Pacific Forum as well as David Lange. Lange's observation that the chairman was appointed not by the Forum leaders but by the board of directors was correct, but his barbed comments were designed for the cut and thrust of New Zealand domestic politics rather than Pacific diplomacy.

In the wider context, Harry Julian's move was appropriate because of the considerable diplomatic and political dimensions of his appointment. As chairman he had cultivated considerable support for the Forum Line from Island leaders.[189] Ratu Sir Kamisese Mara acknowledged this, saying he was 'shattered' by Julian's removal and acknowledging that the chairman had been the main reason for Fiji's decision to become a major supporter of PFL.[190]

The Labour government possessed a considerable mandate and quickly committed itself to deregulation. This was to impact heavily on maritime transport, where PFL was an obvious target for reform-minded officials. By the end of August 1984 the New Zealand Treasury had prepared a paper on the Forum Line which went far beyond the brief to comment on the extension of the line's overdraft from NZ$5.2 million to NZ$6 million.[191] In a wide-ranging report, the Treasury recommended that the overdraft should not be renewed since it regarded PFL as neither necessary nor viable and had considerable sympathy for the Australian position. It argued that the service was more sophisticated than could be justified by commercial considerations and that Island governments should be encouraged to look at alternative uses for their aid money. If PFL was removed other operators would take over, and if there was a resulting shipping shortage, the New Zealand government should look at subsidising private operators. Even if PFL became profitable, the operation could not produce a return on the capital already expended. Treasury officials estimated in March 1984 that New Zealand's contribution to PFL amounted to NZ$44.4 million. This included the cost of the charter subsidy on the New Zealand vessel, which had not previously been included in PFL evaluations and made up more than half of the total.

It was clear that the New Zealand Treasury would oppose any further substantial grants to PFL and would prefer the government to cease its involvement in shipping. An alternative position was that PFL should operate commercially, with no political involvement. To reinforce this, officials quoted the 1979 Carr report, which emphasised that:

> If commercialism is to be dominated by political motivation . . . no amount of consultants, managers or modern vessels will be able to arrest the ceaseless requests for additional finance from all available sources.[192]

However, Treasury had focused solely on technical and economic efficiency issues and avoided practicalities. New Zealand was only one of ten equal shareholders, none of which could make major policy decisions without a majority support of others. The report highlighted the finance New Zealand had already contributed, but disregarded the political, strategic, and industrial relations climate prevailing over the preceding twenty years.

The Fua Kavenga *in dry dock at Auckland.*

It does not seem likely that the New Zealand government seriously considered 'pulling the plug'[193] and, even if that had been the political will, it would have had to gain shareholder support for the move. However, the Treasury position reflected a changing political agenda, in which PFL was being pushed towards a solely commercial focus and possible privatisation.

One of the positive results of the 'more-market' philosophy was warmly embraced by John MacLennan when he succeeded Julian as general manager. Management and board were largely freed to develop the Forum Line within the scope of its existing assets and liabilities, and the fact that it was now profitable put them in a much stronger commercial position—albeit one in which there was no longer the comfort of a shareholder bail-out.

Unfortunately, the new political context constrained management in pursuing one of its initial goals, that of supplying service to small Island states not provided for by commercial carriers. PFL maintained the subsidised feeder service to Kiribati and Tuvalu only because it was financed by donor governments as an aid project managed by PFL. However, when the Australian and New Zealand governments signalled their desire to remove this subsidy, PFL was forced to examine the operation very carefully.

John MacLennan (seated fourth from left) and PFL management team 1989.

Shares

A further positive consequence of capitalisation was that the Forum Line now had a dollar value. During its formative years it had been maintained by shareholder cash injections but was technically insolvent. Capitalisation now provided an asset base against which it could borrow. The original distribution of shares among the shareholder governments had been carefully undertaken. Under usual commercial practice, New Zealand would have taken shares commensurate with the amount of capital it had invested. However New Zealand was conscious that it could have attracted criticism for its degree of influence. To avoid this New Zealand money was ascribed to debt and the two other states most supportive during the recapitalisation were allocated shares that reflected their contributions.

Member Government	'A' Ordinary Shares	Prior to EIB Package (WS$)	Result of EIB Package	Total WS$
Cook Islands	10,000	25,917	29,000	64,917
Fiji	10,000		4, 602, 504	4,612,504
Kiribati	10,000	134, 293	512,056	656,349
Nauru	10,000			10,000
New Zealand	10,000	318,000		328,000
Papua New Guinea	10,000	1,237,698	4,608,471	5,856,169
Solomon Islands	10,000	53,930		63,930
Tonga	10,000	353,327	822,862	1,186,189
Tuvalu	10,000	90,000	316,957	416,957
Samoa	10,000	594,674	862,385	1,467,059
TOTAL	**100,000**	**2,807,839**	**11,754,235**	**14,662,074**[194]

At an Extraordinary General Meeting held at the headquarters of the South Pacific Bureau for Economic Co-operation on 5 December 1985, shareholders voted to raise the nominal NZ$100,000 capital of the New Zealand subsidiary PFL (NZ) Ltd in line with the recapitalisation. The meeting created 19,900,000 new 'B' (non-voting) shares. The distribution of these was in accordance with what had been agreed for PFL's main company and left Papua New Guinea the largest shareholder, followed by Fiji.

The market-driven reduction in vessel charter rates greatly aided PFL's financial position but created continuing tension between the vessel-owning countries and the line. Although all directors recognised the need for the line to operate commercially, the charter rates remained controversial, particularly for the Island vessel owners—Samoa and Tonga. Considerable protest from these governments was supported by the West German government through their representatives, Hamburg Süd. All shareholders agreed that charter rates should be set in accordance with prevailing market conditions. What was at issue was how to move to such a market rate without unreasonable stress being placed on the Tongan and Samoan economies.

There was a tentative revision of the rates in early 1984 to US$3500 per day and this was increased to US$3700 on 4 December 1984 for 1984–85. When rates were due for re-negotiation in early 1986, Island owners and the West German government argued that Samoa and Tonga had been forced to carry too much of the risk and that the rates were too low to service the loan—despite the concessions West Germany had made on capital repayments. The situation for Samoa was particularly grave as it was seeking to re-schedule its external debt. PFL countered by arguing that crewing costs— particularly the cost of the West German officers— were excessive.[195] The 1986 rates were set at US$4000 but PFL management believed that, even at that rate, they were too high. The settlement culminated with the line advising the owners that the vessels' charters would cease on 30 June 1988—a position endorsed by the shareholders' meeting in Suva on 2 September 1987.[196]

This dispute was resolved only with some very careful negotiation. The PFL board called an Extraordinary General Meeting in Rarotonga on 20 November 1987, at a time when Samoa was on the verge of being unable to make its December 1987 loan repayment. The settlement was brokered by Julian's replacement, Labour-appointed director, Michael Hirschfeld. The 1987 charter rate was retrospectively raised to US$4000, while the 1988 rate was set at US$4350. The line offered to pay a contribution to the next docking and annual survey for both vessels and a cash settlement which helped Samoa meet its immediate commitments. In return, however, the shipowners had to accept that all future charter settlements would be commercial propositions in which each owner and PFL accepted the risk inherent in their interest.[197] The charter for *Forum New Zealand II* was left slightly out of kilter at US$4223—lower than for the other two ships, despite the fact that she was a larger, more sophisticated vessel. This anomaly was due for removal in the next charter round.

The *Forum New Zealand II* Purchase

In its first decade, all PFL's vessels had been chartered. By 1989 the line was able to consider purchasing its own. While the New Zealand–Fiji trade had always been the best source of freight, there was considerable potential for growth in the New Zealand–Papua New Guinea trade. Prior to PFL's formation, shipping to Papua New Guinea had been unreliably provided by the Columbus Line and Sofrana Unilines. PFL introduced its service in 1978 operating the *Tauloto II* through Fiji, Tuvalu, Kiribati, the Solomons, Papua New Guinea and back to New Zealand.

Forum Samoa, PFL's first container vessel, was on the run from late 1979, but a year later cargo volumes to Papua New Guinea had increased to such an extent that greater reefer capacity was needed. It was decided to replace *Forum Samoa* with

Forum New Zealand because of her greater size and flexibility and her capacity for 330 refrigerated containers.

Although initially the Papua New Guinea service went via Fiji to provide consistent freight revenue, this was no longer feasible by mid-1992 because the demand for space for Papua New Guinea alone outstripped capacity.

In October 1982 PFL introduced a southbound link from Brisbane to New Zealand and were surprised by the volume of trans-Tasman and Papua New Guinea trade picked up from Australian exporters. When expansion was such that there was enough business for a larger vessel but insufficient for two vessels,[198] management put a proposal to the New Zealand government for a new vessel.

In May 1986 New Zealand agreed to the PFL proposal for a larger vessel, although it subsequently proved impossible to charter a suitable ship. As the only suitable replacement—the *Brabant*—was for sale, New Zealand agreed to the purchase, with the proviso that the subsidy on the new vessel was to be the same as, or lower than, that payable on the original vessel. To achieve this, New Zealand made a one-off contribution of NZ$3.168 million towards upgrading the *Brabant* as the *Forum*

The Forum New Zealand II *was considerably larger and faster than PFL's other vessels.*

New Zealand II. PFL continued to pay the *Forum New Zealand* rate of US$4223 per day for *Forum New Zealand II* and also contributed NZ$1.126 million towards the one-off costs of upgrading.

The total cost of the *Brabant* modifications and delivery was almost twice the original estimate. To avoid the kind of open-ended cost-plus formula which had been a feature of previous arrangements between PFL and the Shipping Corporation of New Zealand, officials sought the corporation's agreement to fund the operation on a time-charter basis. However, the charter rate suggested by the corporation was considerably higher than PFL had anticipated and negotiations stalled. An interim agreement was reached but discussions continued.[199]

The Shipping Corporation of New Zealand had been struggling to reduce its operating losses in order to attain a position where it could be sold. A change in its board membership created a sense of urgency. All members, including Shipping Corporation chairman and PFL director Michael Hirschfeld, were replaced with a new board whose primary role was to prepare the corporation for sale.[200] However, the Shipping Corporation's cashflow was so poor that it could not afford to make employees redundant. Relations with unions, particularly the Merchant Service

Forum New Zealand II ran aground at Lyttelton Heads late in 1988. At the time there was a proposal to stretch the Fua Kavenga *to increase her cargo capacity.*

Guild, were strained to the point that a court injunction was needed in November 1988 to get the *New Zealand Mariner* and *New Zealand Pacific*, to sea.

The unions, aware that a sale was likely, commenced a campaign to convince public opinion that the New Zealand government should retain the corporation. The pressure on Shipping Corporation management showed when, on 9 January 1989, it announced its intention to reflag the *Forum New Zealand II* and the *New Zealand Pacific*. Such a drastic move guaranteed industrial action.

The *New Zealand Pacific* had been diverted to Tahiti on 10 January 1989 and the New Zealand crew replaced. Two days later, when the *Forum New Zealand II* crew arrived in Port Moresby, they were immediately confronted with an ultimatum to accept the Shipping Corporation's new 'international' crewing policy or leave the ship and be replaced by British officers and a Vanuatuan crew. The crew of the *Weka* (as the *Forum New Zealand II* had been renamed in transit) signed, while the officers walked off. By staying with the ship the men were pinning their hopes on court action to have the move declared invalid.[201] Dave Morgan of the Seamen's Union made it clear that he did not want a repetition of the re-crewing of the *New Zealand Pacific*.

The Shipping Corporation of New Zealand *reflagged* Forum New Zealand II *as the* Weka *and the* New Zealand Pacific *as the* Tui *in early 1989.*

In late 1997 he recalled that the *Weka* dispute:

> was settled long before the *Tui*—the *New Zealand Pacific*—because
> of one thing—good communications. We were in communication
> with the crew of the *Weka*. I said sign whatever you like, sign
> whatever they put in front of you. So all the guys signed the
> contracts saying they would take less money, less leave and bow
> every time they went past or something—and they signed and the
> officers didn't—and scab officers came on board. . . . we had
> actually been telling our crews that for some time in the Shipping
> Corporation. Do not surrender the ship under any circum-
> stances.[202]

Forum New Zealand II was reflagged to the Hong Kong-owned Eckington Ltd and
both vessels were managed by Denholm Ship Management Ltd, which was
represented in New Zealand by a senior executive, Gavin Rosser.

The Shipping Corporation estimated that re-crewing could save them NZ$11.6
million per annum, and certainly crew numbers on the *Weka* fell from 26 to 21.
However, the repercussions were considerable. At the end of January 1989, the
Seamen's Union, Cooks and Stewards' Union and Merchant Service Guild took the

Forum New Zealand II *officers left the vessel immediately.*

Shipping Corporation to the Labour Court over the legality of the reflagging. The judge determined that despite the legal moves taken with regard to the ownership and management changes, the ships were still effectively in the control of the Shipping Corporation and, as such, the reflagging to Hong Kong was 'a sham'.[203]

The reflagging caught New Zealand Foreign Affairs staff off guard. Had the Vanuatuan crew gone on board, the ministry would have been faced with providing overseas development aid for a vessel crewed by Islanders. Such an outcome would have severely undermined the political and industrial relations consensus upon which PFL was based. As it was, the immediate industrial conflict had a serious impact on PFL but management's quick action avoided more serious consequences. Yet, at the same time, they negotiated lower crew numbers.

Political intervention saved PFL from becoming further embroiled in a potentially difficult dispute. New Zealand Associate Minister of Foreign Affairs Fran Wilde was a long-time friend of PFL director Michael Hirschfeld and liaised closely with him. She wrote to PFL emphasising that while government aid monies could be redirected to help purchase the *Weka*, they would only be available once PFL had

Eckington Ltd claimed NZ$11 million from the dismissed maritime ratings who remained on board the Weka, *accusing them of barratry — an ancient legal concept which means 'a fraudulent practice committed by the master or crew of a ship to the prejudice of the owner.' The attempt proved unsuccessful.*

signed with the relevant unions a manning and conditions agreement which approximated to international standards.[204] This meant reducing crew numbers and leave provisions considerably below the current norm on the trans-Tasman.

The New Zealand unions, although buoyed by their success at the Labour Court, had been shaken by the Shipping Corporation tactics and the imminent sale. Early in March 1989 they negotiated an agreement which appealed to the government because it removed the need for the Overseas Development Aid (ODA) time charter subsidy. Foreign Affairs relayed the message to its Pacific posts: 'For your information only, the sale of the *Weka* has also terminated the ODA-subsidised time charter with SCONZ and thus saved the ODA programme an estimated NZ$7 million over the remainder of the charter period.'[205]

The purchase of its first vessel was a considerable step for PFL, emphasising the move from under-capitalisation and loss-making to profitability. However, this mark of maturity was undermined by the fact that its timing was not determined by the Forum Line, but was a consequence of political action elsewhere.

The PFL board were grateful for the New Zealand Labour government's NZ$4.874 million assistance with the *Forum New Zealand II* purchase. They were

The re-naming of Forum New Zealand II *as the* Weka *left many bewildered.*

also conscious that New Zealand's contribution and commitment to the line were not fully represented in the shareholding and that the New Zealand bond to subsidise the operation of a New Zealand vessel terminated with the purchase of the *Forum New Zealand II*. It was agreed that to strengthen the regional base of the line, New Zealand capital would be converted into 'C' shares which would hold no dividend until they were converted into 'B' shares on 30 June 1996.

New Zealand received 450,000 of the new shares, while 750,000 were equally distributed among remaining shareholders. A further 187,500 'C' shares were left available for further distribution to Forum countries not currently shareholders. This arrangement increased PFL's capital to reflect its asset base yet retained the ranking of the relative shareholders, of whom New Zealand remained the third largest behind Papua New Guinea and Fiji.[206]

Agencies and Slot Charters

As early as April 1982, PFL had begun to internalise its agency operations. It established its first agency and stevedoring service in Apia, partly to recompense Apia for the relocation of the PFL head office to Auckland but also as recognition that PFL was the major carrier to Samoa. This agency was a new operation running in competition with the former agent, Union Maritime Services.[207]

By acting as agents for their own freight and providing service to other companies, PFL profitably integrated new business within its organisation so that by 1984, at the end of the five-year agency agreement with Union Maritime Services for the South Pacific trade, PFL indicated that it would not renew the contract.

In July 1985 PFL established its own agency for this trade and in the following year ended its agency agreement with the Shipping Corporation of New Zealand on the central South Pacific route. In late 1985 it had purchased Akarana Freight (NZ) to provide a stevedoring operation which later extended to a capacity to pack LCL (less than container load) freight. Such a capacity was significant in trade with the Islands, where freight movements were small and often included the transportation of personal effects. These changes made PFL self-reliant in its main port.

Suva was the first Island agency outside Apia. This was fitting since it was PFL's largest port of call and an important source of freight in its own right, as well as a trans-shipment point from smaller islands. By May 1989 PFL purchased Union Maritime Services Fiji, whose Lautoka office became part of the PFL network, while the Suva offices were amalgamated. The Forum Line's Pacific representation was largely completed when, in August 1989, it acquired Union Maritime Services in Apia, where the ship agency functions (including a profitable travel agency) were combined with the PFL structure. When PFL's Auckland office moved to Anzac Avenue in August 1987, it was decided to establish the ship agency as a separate division—Forum Shipping Agencies International (FSAI)—to co-ordinate day-to-day freight collection and movements.

Such developments were a logical extension of PFL business and in accordance with the 1977 Memorandum of Understanding. PFL adopted other commercial strategies to expand its business, some of which saw the line diversify into non-traditional trade areas. In the early 1980s PFL had moved into the trans-Tasman trade with calls to Brisbane. This had grown quickly, although at times competition, a lack of space on vessels, or restrictions placed on PFL by the maritime unions' trans-Tasman Accord meant that it had to adapt its service to meet new requirements. *Forum New Zealand II*, with her greater freight capacity, allowed PFL to reinstate the route from Brisbane to New Zealand in March 1987. Later that year the line had developed sufficient trade to be able to terminate the New Zealand Line slot charter on the New Zealand–Brisbane trade. For the first time PFL independently operated a trans-Tasman service in both directions.[208]

Inevitably, success drew competitors onto the Brisbane run and PFL had to rationalise its service. PFL and the Australian National Line agreed to establish a joint-venture ship agency in New Zealand, creating a clever acronym—FAST (the Forum ANL Shipping and Transport Agency). Forum Line agency offices at Auckland and Christchurch changed their names and were strengthened to cope with the increased workload. An office was also opened in Wellington, while an owners' representative was appointed in Brisbane to service the Brisbane–Papua New Guinea trade.

Competition on the Australia, New Caledonia and Fiji routes had been intense in the mid-1980s, to the extent that most operators were losing money. In late 1987 PFL and Sofrana (Aust.) formed a joint venture to New Caledonia and Fiji called the Pacific Express Line. This joint venture operated for only six months before it was terminated to make way for wider co-operation. In July 1988 shipowners, recognising the problem, met to discuss potential solutions. Associated Container Transportation (Australia) Ltd, PFL, Sofrana, Compagnie Générale Maritime and the APIL consortium* reached an agreement on co-operation which effectively eased the downward pressure on freight rates.

The Weka *at Lyttelton in 1989.*

*See list of abbreviations page ix.

Pacific Forum Line

Offices & Agents

Offices

Pacific Forum Line (NZ) Ltd
49-55 Anzac Avenue
P.O. Box 796
Auckland 1. New Zealand
Ph (09) 396-700
Telex NZFORUM 60460
Fax (09) 392-683

Pacific Forum Line
187 Rodwell Road
P.O. Box 13-147,
Suva, Fiji.
Ph 315-444 (4 lines)
Telex PACFORUM FJ2429
Fax 312-130

Pacific Forum Line
Beach Road, Matautu-tai,
P.O. Box 655, Apia,
Western Samoa
Ph 20-345/6/7/8, 24-445
Telex FORUML 234
Fax 22-343

Agents

American Samoa
Pago Pago Polynesian Shipping Services
P.O. Box 1478,
American Samoa 96799.
Ph. 633-1211/12/13
Telex POLYSHIPS SB 514
Fax 633-2073

Australia
Sydney Union-Bulkships
333-339 George Street,
G.P.O. Box 534
Australia 2001.
Ph. 20-238
Telex SHIPS AA 20397
Fax 290 1610

Brisbane Union-Bulkships
915 Nudgee Road,
G.P.O. Box 2205
Queensland 4014
Ph. 267-6344.
Telex SHIPS AA 40584
Fax 267 6644

Melbourne Union-Bulkships
114 William Street
G.P.O. Box 1275L
Victoria 3001
Ph 609-1011.
Telex SHIPS AA 30098
Fax 670 1784

Adelaide Union-Bulkships
259 St. Vincent Street,
G.P.O. Box 162
South Australia 5015
Ph. 47-1633
Telex SHIPS AA 82099
Fax 2400 552

Fremantle Union-Bulkships
17 Henry Street,
P.O. Box 434,
West Australia 6160
Ph. 335-1091
Telex SHIPS AA 92136
Fax 3361 774

Fiji
Lautoka Union Maritime Services
Limited
177 Vitogo Parade,
P.O. Box 49.
Ph. 60-577, 60-752.
Telex UNION FJ 5158
Fax 62-985

Suva Forum Shipping Agencies
refer Pacific Forum Line,
Suva, above.

Kiribati
Tarawa Shipping Corporation of
Kiribati
P.O. Box 495, Betio.
Ph 26-195
Telex KI 77030 SCK BETIO

New Caledonia
Noumea Sofrana Unilines
Avenue James Cook
P.O. Box 1602
Ph. 27 51 91
Telex 3048 NM
Fax 27 26 11

New Zealand
Auckland Forum Shipping Agencies
International
refer Pacific Forum Line (NZ)
Ltd, Auckland, above.

Napier C.A. Olsen Limited
10 Bower Street,
P.O. Box 542
Ph 351-913
Telex OLSENCO NZ32049
Fax 51-250

Wellington Seabridge New Zealand
110 Featherston Street
P.O. Box 652
Ph 722 483
Telex 31194
Fax 722 117

Christchurch/
Lyttelton Forum Shipping Agencies
International — Christchurch
6th Floor, Manchester Court
160 Manchester Street
P.O. Box 1180
Ph 57 701
Telex 40145 CHFORUM
Fax 57 157

Papua New Guinea
Port Moresby
Steamships Shipping &
Transport
Stanley Esplanade
P.O. Box 634 Ph 220-283
Telex STEAMOS NE 22198
Fax 213-595

Lae Steamships Shipping &
Transport
Milfordhaven Road
P.O. Box 1822
Ph 425-444
Telex STEAM NE 42423
Fax 425-194

PNG Secondary Ports
Steamships Shipping and
Transport

Solomon Islands
Honiara Sullivans (Solomon Is) Limited
Dowling Drive,
G.P.O. Box 3
Ph. 21-643.
Telex CHASULL HQ 66318
Fax 23-860

Tahiti
Papeete Compagnie Maritime
Polyne 'Sienne
P.O. Box 368
Ph 428-307
Telex 258 FP

Tonga
Nuku'alofa Union Maritime Services
Limited
Taufa'ahau Road
P.O. Box 4
Ph 21-644, 21-645
Telex UNIONCO TS66227
Fax 22-970

Tuvalu
Funafuti Tuvalu Cooperative
Vaiaku.

Vanuatu
Port Villa Vila Agents Limited
Kumul Highway
P.O. Box 62
Ph 2490
Telex 1044 VILAGE
Fax 3379

Western Samoa
Apia Forum Shipping Agencies
refer Pacific Form Line,
Apia, above.

PFL's offices and agents in 1989.

The Purchase of *Forum Papua New Guinea*

By 1989 PFL had enjoyed four profitable years and purchased its first vessel. During that year management became concerned that the central Pacific service, operating from New Zealand via Brisbane to Papua New Guinea and the Solomons, was vulnerable to competition. The one-ship operation had a passage time in excess of 45 days and there was considerable demand for a more frequent service. Management and various consultants carried out financial analyses which showed that PFL should purchase or charter a second vessel. This was possible as shareholders had left funds in the line.

As charter rates were extremely high, PFL seriously considered purchasing. However, financial models tested by Touche Ross demonstrated that the purchase of another vessel would produce losses between 1990 and 1992—although following this, trade growth seemed likely to sustain the increased costs.

By late 1989 PFL had examined on paper some 150 vessels and from three choices selected the *Star Siranger*—a vessel capable of carrying both bulk and container cargoes. She was targeted at capturing the Papua New Guinea bulk cargo trade.

After survey, the vessel was brought to New Zealand for minor modifications before being introduced into service in July 1990. Renamed *Forum Papua New Guinea*, she cost NZ$18,207,788, which was funded from the line's own resources and through a NZ$10 million loan from the State Bank of South Australia. Her purchase was significant because it was strictly commercial and was financed conventionally by a bank loan based on PFL's assets.

At the beginning of 1989 PFL had chartered all its vessels. By mid-1990 it owned two large ships and was responsible for their crewing, maintenance and insurance. Pacific Forum Line (NZ) Ltd established a separate division to manage them. The division's services were also offered to other vessel operators, particularly New Zealand Steel for the management of their vessel, the *Pioneer Tween*.

The Forum Papua New Guinea *at Lyttelton in 1990.*

CHAPTER FIVE

The Feeder Service

TUVALU AND KIRIBATI became independent in 1978 and 1979. The isolation of these tiny resource-poor states made trade development very difficult and imports expensive. Neither had reliable shipping services and both regarded PFL as a possible solution to their problem. In search of shipping aid they approached PFL as well as the Australian and New Zealand governments. Tuvalu highlighted its position as a PFL shareholder in order to further its case for support and indicated its intention to ask Australia for a direct subsidy if New Zealand or PFL could not help.[209]

PFL had initially included Tarawa and Funafuti in its services but quickly abandoned them because of insufficient patronage. New Zealand attempted to assist by moving the *Benjamin Bowring*—a vessel which had been used in the Tokelaus— to a feeder route based in Fiji. This was not envisaged as permanent and ended in November 1980 when the charter expired. Hopes that commercial operators would develop a service were not fulfilled.[210] A second vessel, the *Ai Sokula*, was chartered the following year but had just been placed on the run when she ran aground and was severely damaged. There were no resources left for a replacement and Tuvalu, in particular, faced a considerable period without a ship calling at its main port.[211]

Australia was reluctant to subsidise competition for commercial shipping operators. Advice available to Canberra about the problems faced by Tuvalu and Kiribati differed from Wellington's in that it emphasised the infrastructural problems for commercial operators. Tuvalu, while appreciative of PFL's intention to promote a Suva-based feeder service, preferred a direct link ex-Sydney. Karlander established this in late 1981 while Kiribati was seeking to increase the frequency of the *Moana Raoi*'s Sydney–Tarawa–Funafuti run from three-monthly to six-weekly. Australian officials believed that Kiribati leaders were then satisfied with the visits they received from Karlander ex-Sydney and the Kyowa Line ex-Auckland.[212]

One reason for Ratu Sir Kamisese Mara's early reluctance to give the Pacific Forum Line full support had been its unwillingness to provide non-commercial services. He had made this explicit at the 1981 Forum at Port Vila, saying that he would consider further support for PFL only when it fulfilled that aspect of the Memorandum of Understanding. Ratu Mara's insistence related in part to his own country's needs. 'I can speak with experience because it does not pay to have ships from my part of Fiji, but we always insist that ships are sent there.'[213]

At New Delhi Australia stated that it believed aid in the form of shipping services could be most appropriately distributed by distinct subsidies to private operators rather than to the regional line. When Tuvalu and Kiribati approached New Zealand about the possibility of supporting a PFL service to their ports,[214] New Zealand consulted Australia. The OECD's Developmental Aid Commission had recently reclassified New Zealand's shipping assistance as overseas development aid and this may have facilitated the agreement to subsidise a service, although Australia remained suspicious of PFL and insisted that separate accounts be kept for the feeder service.

PFL received a subsidy to run the Kiribati government's *Moana Raoi*[215] from Fiji to Kiribati and Tuvalu.[216] This service was established in 1982 on the basis of an initial joint New Zealand-Australian grant of US$300,000 which was sufficient to maintain operations until mid-1985.[217] This was the result of the Kiribati Shipping Corporation's willingness to accept a voyage charter, PFL management's decision at the outset to provide a one-vessel service and good patronage by local exporters in Kiribati and Tuvalu. New Zealand and Australia confirmed in 1985 that they would continue to fund the service until the end of 1987.

Kiribati and Tuvalu had differing needs. Tuvalu had no other shipping link and, without this feeder service, would have been dependent on irregular visits by any vessel which could be persuaded to call. Kiribati, on the other hand, had the commercial operator Container Chief Services (Swires) servicing its two main export industries—copra and fishing. However, it was also considerably to the Kiribati government's advantage that PFL should charter their vessel on a regular basis. New Zealand officials were particularly keen that Kiribati make significant use of the service in order to minimise losses.

The Moana Raoi *service from Suva operated from 1982 to 1988.*

While PFL provided contact with the outside world, Kiribati and Tuvalu desired direct links with Australia and New Zealand rather than expensive, slow transshipment via Suva. There were also pilferage problems with the *Moana Raoi*'s conventional cargo. Tuvalu's Minister of Finance, N. F. Naisali, expressed appreciation for the PFL service but also frustration that Tuvalu had had no direct ship visit from either Australia or New Zealand between July and November 1985. As a consequence there were shortages of some food items.[218]

Repeated investigations into shipping to the two small states revealed its precarious nature and the importance of maintaining the service. However, Kiribati officials were equally keen to maintain their direct links with Australia and reluctant to make a definitive commitment to PFL. Using the *Moana Raoi*, PFL earned approximately NZ$100,000 per trip but she was often unavailable because the Kiribati government was using her. If PFL hired Kiribati's smaller vessel, the earnings were less and costs similar.[219]

Even when available, the *Moana Raoi* was merely a temporary solution to Tuvalu's shipping problems. She was already over 30 years old and coming up for replacement. On his retirement from PFL, George Fulcher undertook a pre-

Built in 1958, the Kiribati government's conventional Moana Raoi *was chartered for the Tuvalu and Kiribati feeder service.*

feasibility study of extending the feeder service into Micronesia. This showed that the profitability of any extension would be at best marginal, even with the continued subsidy. However, an appropriately designed, purpose-built vessel was far more likely to prove satisfactory than a conventional vessel or a small container ship. A decision was required without delay since PFL had to find a replacement for the *Moana Raoi*, which was now out of 'class'.

Management spent much time and effort looking for a cost-effective alternative which would improve the service to the Islands.[220] If it was to aim for extending the service into Micronesia and wanted to be competitive, PFL had to consider a containerised service.[221]

Initially it was hoped that Lomé III monies could be used to purchase a suitable vessel. In Apia in April 1988, during the joint meeting of the African, Caribbean

The 85-TEU container vessel Forum Micronesia *used on the feeder service from 1988 to 1993.*

and Pacific Group with the European Community, it was agreed that Lomé III funds could cover partial financing of a purpose-built vessel for the PFL feeder service. A feasibility study concluded that such a vessel would cost around ECU11,000,000. Rather than commit funds at this stage, European Community officials chose to await the results of the initial *Forum Micronesia* charter. In the interim the Japanese government also expressed interest in providing a new vessel although this did not amount to a firm offer.[222] Rather than lose access to the Lomé funds, the Forum Line investigated the purchase of more containers. However, it soon became clear that the economic return on this was insufficient for a viable loan, and shareholder governments were no longer interested in guaranteeing these.

Australian aid officials, already suspicious of New Zealand motives in funding the feeder service, had considerable difficulty with the proposal to extend it to Micronesia. They argued that export opportunities for Australia had been lost with the introduction of the current feeder service and that imports for Kiribati and Tuvalu were increasingly sourced from Suva, often without regard to country of origin. Decreased business meant a reduction of direct shipping from Australian ports to these areas and an extended feeder service might harm Australian trade with Micronesia.[223]

In late 1988 PFL decided to upgrade the feeder service since the *Moana Raoi* had failed to gain an international certificate. The small 120-container capacity *Forum Micronesia* was chartered to establish a run which, it was recognised, would probably not be profitable. However, it seemed possible to operate at a cost similar to that of running the *Moana Raoi*, while the containerised trade would be an improvement on what it replaced.[224]

To achieve viability, *Forum Micronesia*'s schedules changed frequently. In April 1989 she operated an Auckland–Suva–Funafuti–Tarawa–Majuro (Marshall Islands) route but this was quickly changed to a Fiji-based service offering trans-shipment to Auckland. The amended route was maintained from May 1990 until December 1991 and, for a brief period, included Nauru. At this time PFL served all of its shareholder governments, which was a considerable testament to its commitment to the welfare of isolated Island economies. However, the Nauru and Majuro service was not heavily patronised, overall freight volumes declined considerably and the entire operation needed to be rethought. It had proved particularly difficult to retain consistent cargoes from Kiribati. Both Nauru and Majuro were dropped from the run and then in December 1991 the service reverted to a round trip from Fiji to Funafuti and Tarawa.

Funding a purpose-built vessel was again investigated in the Lomé IV round in 1992. PFL put considerable effort into acquiring aid money to build an appropriate vessel and the Australian government was even prepared to give support if PFL could secure Lomé funds. Unfortunately a new feasibility study showed that the economic prospects of such a service had declined and the European Community decided not to recommend further funding.[225]

In July 1992, when the Hawaii Pacific Line ceased its operations to Hawaii, PFL hoped that this would boost the flagging fortunes of a service which could not long continue while the subsidy and the earnings were not covering costs. Although now profitable, PFL could not afford such depletion of its capital reserves.

The new schedule was an ambitious attempt to link profitable and unprofitable sectors. The 40-day round trip from Fiji included Hawaii, the two Samoas, Tonga, Kiribati and Tuvalu.[226] Unfortunately freight out of Honolulu did not live up to expectations. PFL had come to the end of a five-year period of profitability in its other operations and management, conscious that the service was incurring losses, had little choice but to abandon it.

The PFL board were particularly unhappy with the negative conclusions of the second Lomé report into the viability of the feeder service. The Majuro representa-

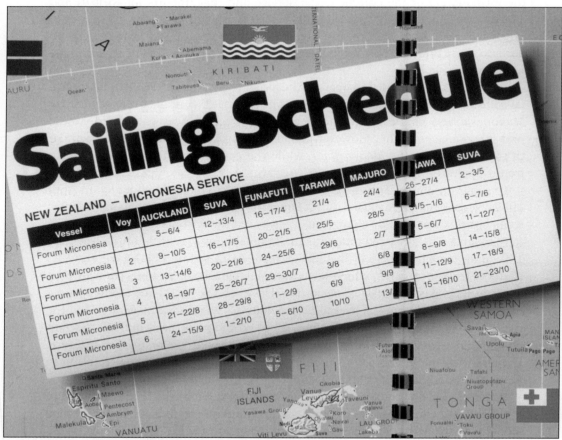

Sailing Schedule

NEW ZEALAND – MICRONESIA SERVICE

Vessel	Voy	AUCKLAND	SUVA	FUNAFUTI	TARAWA	MAJURO	TARAWA	SUVA
					21/4	24/4	26–27/4	2–3/5
Forum Micronesia	1	5–6/4	12–13/4	16–17/4	25/5	28/5	31/5–1/6	6–7/6
Forum Micronesia	2	9–10/5	16–17/5	20–21/5	29/6	2/7	5–6/7	11–12/7
Forum Micronesia	3	13–14/6	20–21/6	24–25/6	3/8	6/8	8–9/8	14–15/8
Forum Micronesia	4	18–19/7	25–26/7	29–30/7	6/9	9/9	11–12/9	17–18/9
Forum Micronesia	5	21–22/8	28–29/8	1–2/9	10/10	13/	15–16/10	21–23/10
Forum Micronesia	6	24–15/9	1–2/10	5–6/10				

The feeder service schedule at its height as advertised in PFL's 1992 brochure.

tive was not at the meeting, but the Tuvalu representative agreed that the service should be terminated. The New Zealand High Commissioner in Suva was also concerned that Australian-based Container Chief Services was not willing to alter its Australia–Kiribati operation to call at Tuvalu. In early March 1993 he commented that:

> This morning's decision was undoubtedly the right one for PFL. But it has not solved the substantive problem, namely the provision of adequate shipping services to Tuvalu (and to a lesser extent to Kiribati). It has simply shifted the problem away from PFL, and if Tuvalu is not able to reach an agreement with a shipper in the very near future we can expect to be asked to assist in some way. We would also expect the issue to arise at the next Maritime Committee and council meeting in Tonga . . .[227]

The feeder service failed for several reasons. It was simply not possible to continue an uneconomic operation for any length of time without damage to PFL's wider prospects. It was also impossible to include Tuvalu and Kiribati on the routes of the larger vessels, while to revert to break-bulk conventional cargo was neither practical nor financially sound. There had been technical problems with the feeder service as established. *Forum Micronesia* displayed many of the problems of smaller container vessels, being slow and costly to run. Honolulu proved an expensive port of call and cargo south to the Pacific Islands was limited.

The service was further hit by currency fluctuations. Costs were mainly in US dollars but the aid subsidies and earnings were in the weaker Australian and New Zealand currencies. The projected loss for 1992—NZ$1,836,335—was unsustainable. Kiribati had come to rely more on the Swires service than on PFL and, while Tuvalu was vulnerable, there was insufficient trade to offset the losses.[228]

The demise of the feeder service underlined the tension between two of PFL's core objectives in the 1977 Memorandum of Understanding—to provide service to isolated Pacific Islands and to be a self-sufficient, profitable commercial operation. The reluctance of New Zealand and Australia to subsidise the service meant that the only way in which PFL could have maintained the operation was denied to them. For over a decade the line had struggled to maintain and develop a reliable operation. It had run a conventional vessel until the end of her economic life and made an earnest endeavour to make the leap from a conventional to a containerised service.

Capital requirements and infrastructural changes had been an impediment a decade earlier when PFL containerised its main services. Even in the darkest days of 1983, the prospects for PFL's main services were positive. By contrast, the feeder service was always precarious and, without the guarantee of an adequate subsidy, proved ultimately unsustainable.

CHAPTER SIX

Markets and Competition

D URING THE NEW ZEALAND Labour government's second term,
political energy was focused on further reforms, particularly in the
maritime sector, which culminated in the sale of the Shipping Corporation
to private interests in 1989. This was one aspect of a wider push to increase
competition in all sectors since the government required local authorities to
establish port companies, and disestablished the Waterfront Industry Commission
which had co-ordinated the hiring of wharf labour. Industrial unrest arising from
these developments led to a disrupted year for PFL.

In 1989 the Labour government announced the formation of a Shipping Industry
Reform Task Force which was to involve shipowners, seamen and parties with an
interest in cargoes. It soon became apparent that consumer and employer interests
would dominate and that the thrust of the task force's efforts would be to reduce
on-board costs. Its July 1990 report emphasised the need for reductions in crew
numbers, reorganisation of shipboard practices, re-skilling of officers and crews and
an overall focus on international competitiveness.

For PFL, the key recommendation was the removal of the Shipping and Seamen
Act requirement to pay New Zealand award rates to all seamen involved in the
coastal trade. The new National government in 1990 also wanted to allow overseas
operators full access to coastal trade, and the 1994 Marine Transport Act removed
the last legislative impediment to having non-New Zealand crews, including Pacific
Islanders, working New Zealand waters.

However, the major barrier to foreign access to New Zealand ports had always been industrial rather than legislative. The Trans-Tasman Accord between the Australian and New Zealand maritime unions had required companies to employ crews of their respective nationals. This agreement, which dated back to the 1970s—and unofficially much earlier—was challenged in the early 1990s. The possibility of opening up trans-Tasman trade to less expensive crews was potentially very important for PFL because of its service between Brisbane and New Zealand.[229]

If reform created long-term possibilities, there were headaches in the shorter term. Early in 1989 PFL had been involved in disputes arising from the Shipping Corporation's reflagging of *Forum New Zealand II*, but this was only the beginning. Throughout 1989 there was industrial action by the maritime unions in retaliation against the New Zealand government's port reform legislation. These culminated in a five-week stoppage of all New Zealand ports from midnight 30 September.[230] PFL had little choice but to carry the cost of this disruption in the hope that such a showdown would clear the way for greater port efficiency. In the *New Zealand Shipping Gazette* Dave McIntyre highlighted PFL's double dose of industrial action and suggested that the line may have suffered considerably as a result:

PFL on Recovery Course after Reflagging and Port Problems

. . . Pacific Forum Line will be one of those whose results will show some scars from the ports dispute. Where PFL will be worse affected than its contemporaries is that it also suffered tremendous damage at the start of 1989 from the reflagging controversy.

Stranded

You may recall that PFL was the victim when the Shipping Corporation reflagged the *Forum New Zealand II* as the *Weka*. The upshot was that from early February until March 7 last year the ship was stranded in Auckland, blacked by the maritime unions and also left untouched by the harbour board workers

This is where the real damage was done to PFL. For a month the line was out of service on its major Central Pacific Service. It was supposed to be running a five weekly round voyage encompassing Auckland, Lyttelton, Napier, Brisbane, Port Moresby, Lae, Honiara, Brisbane again and Auckland.

Given the hassle of being blacked for a month, basically an entire round trip was lost. During that time customers did not stop manufacturing, importing or shipping. Instead they looked elsewhere.

PFL found its escape route partly through buying the *Forum New Zealand II* and organising a favourable manning and conditions deal with the maritime unions.

I say 'partly' because PFL suffered long-term damage to its standing with clients.[231]

The Star Siranger *at Lyttelton in 1990.*

Despite these industrial problems, directors were still confident of the future. Late in 1989 the board accepted a management plan to strengthen the New Zealand–Papua New Guinea service by purchasing a second vessel, the Norwegian container and bulk carrier, *Star Siranger*. With a total capacity for 636 containers and larger than the *Forum New Zealand II*, it was hoped that the *Forum Papua New Guinea* would capture more of the growing central Pacific trade, particularly in bulk commodities such as coal, cement, sorghum, wheat and sugar.[232]

Forum New Zealand II, *the first vessel owned by PFL, operated on the central Pacific route between New Zealand and Papua New Guinea.*

Dave McIntyre, in the *New Zealand Shipping Gazette* of May 1990, observed:

> The PFL fleet mix now has greater flexibility—something I'll refer
> to again shortly. Markets that appeal include wheat, sugar, stock
> food, tallow and coconut oil.
>
> The second thing to take note of is how this will affect PFL's
> schedule. This is an area where the company has been receiving
> some flak for failing to maintain timetables, so an additional vessel
> on its major service should ease the problem while increasing
> capacity.
>
> **Flexibility Appeal**
>
> This is where the flexibility of having two vessels appeals. The
> *Forum New Zealand*, which is now following generally the same
> port rotation (minus the Fiji call), is intended to run Lyttelton-
> Auckland-Brisbane-Port Moresby-Rabaul-Brisbane-Lyttelton.
>
> The Fiji call usually belongs to the PFL South Pacific trade, but
> the new ship will call in there to take some of the pressure off the
> *Forum Samoa*, which is running to capacity.
>
> The Rabaul call is also new. PFL has previously served the port
> by trans-shipment through Lae, but the advent of a second ship
> plus a trend towards increasing trade means that it can now be
> called direct.
>
> A third area where the new flexibility may show up is in the
> liquid bulk market. If Rabaul, for instance, becomes a liquid bulk
> call, then expect it to be switched to the *Forum Papua New
> Guinea*'s schedule, in a swap with Honiara becoming a destination
> for the other ship.[233]

A second ship purchase was a considerable risk but the board felt confident after
five profitable years.[234] However, the timing proved awkward because PFL's major
competitor, Sofrana, had been taken over by the French shipping conglomerate
Delmas Vieljeux and was refocusing its energies on central Pacific routes.

At the same time, the new Translink Pacific Limited was competing with most
of PFL's services and, although the Warner Pacific Line had faded, another new-
comer, W Island Line, served Auckland, Lyttelton, Suva, Vavau and Nuku'alofa.
In mid-December 1990, Dave McIntyre commented in the *New Zealand Shipping
Gazette*:

> For PFL, the time for making substantial new investments has
> passed. It has its two new vessels. The next year or so will see it
> paying its mortgage, in a trade that is getting tougher.[235]

Projections of small losses after the purchase of the *Forum Papua New Guinea* proved too cautious: there were far greater losses in 1990–91 and 1991–92 than had been anticipated. While the new vessel contributed to a moderate growth in freight, largely in bulk coal, sorghum and tallow, she was tied to the regular Papua New Guinea trade where the anticipated growth did not occur.[236]

There were other problems. PFL's debt had increased as a consequence of the purchase[237] and the Brisbane run was under concerted attack from other trans-Tasman operators,[238] made worse by the arrival of South Pacific Shipping using cheap vessels built under a German tax incentive. Rates on the Tasman plummeted.

Nor were PFL's other routes in a particularly strong position. Trade out of Australia had been unprofitable since the late 1980s. PFL had reacted to this by entering a joint-service pool to New Caledonia and Fiji with Sofrana, Chief Container Services (Swires), Associated Container Transport Australia Ltd and the Compagnie Générale Maritime. Results were positive in that rates had stabilised and PFL faced no significant Australian competition on services to Samoa or Tonga.

The Forum Line further developed its agencies. The Australian National Line and PFL joint agency FAST successfully internalised activities that had proved uneconomic. In June 1991 ANL's managing director, John Bicknell, and PFL's general manager John MacLennan announced the formation of a joint Brisbane service connecting Queensland with major New Zealand ports.[239]

By 1993 it was clear that the difficult trading situation would endure, as would intense competition on all three services. In his 1993 report to shareholders John MacLennan made the alternatives clear:

> The Board has been advised that management cannot identify any immediate relief from the intense competition faced on all routes and services. Thought must be given to developing joint rational-isation of services with one other major operator in the region which, as a partnership, will help combat the effects of competi-tion. At the same time consideration must be given to reduce overheads, which will entail downsizing the fleet. This will in turn reduce debt and provide additional working capital.[240]

Management implemented short- and medium-term strategies to improve the trading position. Freight forwarding activities in New Zealand were redeveloped with the creation of two organisations, Freight Stations Ltd and Freight People. In 1992, in response to the deregulation of port labour, PFL set up its own packing station at the Penrose industrial estate in Auckland. Although facing considerable competition, it gained a greater share of the new market by shipping not only on its own vessels but also on Translink, Sofrana, and Reef Shipping. Consequent growth saw the move to larger premises in Mount Wellington in June 1993. A re-examination of the service led to splitting the division into two operations.

The Price Waterhouse Report

Meanwhile Tuvalu, concerned at the loss of the feeder service, requested an evaluation of the line's performance. The board agreed to commission Price Waterhouse to investigate the company structure and suggest strategies for achieving consistent profitability. This was undertaken using residual finance from the New Zealand subsidy for the Micronesian service.

Price Waterhouse compared PFL with a conventional company and directed criticisms at the line's structure. While such a stance was out of sympathy with the history of PFL's establishment, the report encapsulated many of the arguments in the debate about PFL's commercial orientation. Released to management in November 1994, it has since formed a useful basis for further debate and considerable change.

Price Waterhouse recognised PFL's important role in improving the regional maritime infrastructure, but placed their faith in market forces:

> It could be argued that the existence of PFL in the period after its establishment was a main contributing factor to the achievement of these [regional development] objectives. Currently it can be argued that the competitive market for shipping services in the region has brought about the achievement of those objectives.[241]

The report also highlighted the various non-commercial agendas represented in some shareholders' participation in PFL and argued that these should be discarded:

> Many participants in PFL have considered their investment as an 'insurance policy' to obtain shipping services if the private sector chose not to operate. This study has prompted a review of that approach. In some nations it is considered that the need for PFL to make a profit has taken priority to the Line's stated objective to be an instrument of regional and economic development.[242]

Price Waterhouse pointed out that while PFL's income from freight had been stable, its costs had been erratic. Since 1989, cashflow operating activities had remained at approximately NZ$55 million. However, it was clear that the purchase of the two vessels for the central South Pacific run had not been successful, while the dramatic downturn on the New Zealand–Brisbane–Papua New Guinea service had caused considerable losses. By 1994 the biggest loss factor was voyages, although losses were not equal between routes. The New Zealand–South Pacific trade (Lyttelton, Napier, Auckland, Lautoka, Suva, Apia, Pago Pago and Nuku'alofa) was consistently profitable throughout 1993, although it made a small loss after administrative overheads were deducted. The Australia–South Pacific trade, which had been uneconomic in the early 1990s, was now also profitable.

Nevertheless, the central Pacific trade had produced consistent losses which were not mitigated by a small profit on the joint-venture Brisbane trade.[243] The message from the consultants was clear: the losses on the route had to be turned around, if necessary by a dramatic rethink of the service. This change was a reversal of the 1989 policy to develop the Papua New Guinea run and an acceptance that the strategy had not been successful.

Shortly after the purchase of the *Forum New Zealand II* in 1989 the estimated capital value of the Forum Line had been as high as NZ$41.73 million. By 1994 it had reduced to an estimated NZ$20 million. While such events occur in the shipping industry, PFL had paid no dividends during that time and the loss was absolute.[244]

Price Waterhouse laid considerable emphasis on the opportunity cost of the capital invested in PFL. By the mid-1990s only New Zealand, Australia, Fiji, Papua New Guinea, Samoa and Tonga were serviced by the Forum Line. The other shareholders, including the Solomons, Tuvalu, Kiribati, the Cook Islands, Nauru, the Marshall Islands and Niue, were not.[245] Hence more than half the shareholders were neither benefiting from a shipping service nor receiving dividends on capital invested.

Direct Services 1994

	Shareholders	Non-shareholders
Receive Direct PFL Service	New Zealand Fiji Papua New Guinea Samoa Tonga	Australia
No Direct PFL Service	Solomon Islands Tuvalu Kiribati Cook Islands Nauru Marshall Islands Niue	Federated States of Micronesia Vanuatu

The Forum Line could not look to population growth as a saviour since there was no significant increase projected for the region. Nor was there any real likelihood of sustained growth in intra-regional trade, owing to the similar nature of most Island exports. The continuing pattern of competition in regional shipping was characterised by frequent new entrants and equally frequent withdrawals. While PFL had attained a 30 to 35 per cent market share on its routes there seemed little prospect of improvement, largely because it operated in an industry where it was not possible to differentiate its service sufficiently from that of competitors. Price Waterhouse argued that PFL's position was analogous to that of a commodity producer whose only successful long-term strategy was to reduce operating costs in order to win a price war.[246]

This meant that the Forum Line would always be vulnerable to competitors' price-cutting and would have to focus on being a low-cost commercial operator in a continuously difficult market.

Price Waterhouse strongly recommended the preparation of a strategic plan, to be updated annually, with performance measured by an outside body. Since PFL was jointly owned by Forum governments, it escaped annual audit by any one sovereign state. It should therefore be subject to some form of annual review or audit, as were all New Zealand state-owned enterprises.[247]

Price Waterhouse also suggested structural changes to PFL governance to reflect its commercial re-orientation. This meant the removal of the policy role of the Regional Shipping Council—whereby non-shareholding countries such as Australia, Vanuatu and the Federated States of Micronesia could influence the line's policy. The report also recommended that the Memorandum of Understanding should be amended to remove social objectives and allow PFL to concentrate on making a financial return for its shareholders, while the Articles controlling share transfers should be amended to allow a more normal sale and exchange of shares.

The consultants questioned the method of appointing directors as well as the range of skills represented on the board. In practice they were largely party-political or civil service appointments which changed at least as frequently as the shareholder government and often more so. Price Waterhouse emphasised the need for a continuity in appropriate skills and suggested that appointments should be made to provide these rather than to serve political agendas.

Facing page: The second vessel purchased by PFL, Forum Papua New Guinea, *was a dual-purpose ship capable of carrying containers or bulk cargoes.*

Response to Price Waterhouse

These recommendations were considerable and, if adopted, would significantly alter the political understandings embodied in the Pacific Forum Line. Respective governments had first to decide whether they wished to be involved in shipping. Despite some wavering, most seemed to want to continue with the Forum Line. Some 'free market' elements in the New Zealand government advocated privatisation but what finally appeared to save PFL was the reluctance of other shareholders to privatise, as well as the line's small size and the fact that it had not been a cost to the New Zealand taxpayer in the previous decade.

New Zealand Prime Minister Jim Bolger is reported to have reacted to the suggestion of privatisation by saying, 'If it runs at a loss, then so be it, but let's not get cute on privatisation for the sake of it.' In broader terms there was a concern that if PFL was privatised for whatever reason, there might be pressure on New Zealand to create a new line or increase its aid.

At the time of writing PFL is still in the process of responding to the Price Waterhouse report. In general the board has adopted some of the operational aspects and maintained profitability. In particular it has continued with the rationalisation of the Papua New Guinea service—a process which began before the report was commissioned.

Competition on the New Zealand–Papua New Guinea trade was extreme in the early 1990s. Shipping commentators were surprised that the companies concerned had not sought rationalisation earlier.[248] PFL general manager John MacLennan was certainly aware of the problem and summed up the changes thus:

> In the past you could market a service on its reliability. Today, if you try to market that, it has no effect because there are so many ships around that the shipper can pick and choose.

The Forum Line moved to curtail losses in mid-1993 by allying itself with Sofrana Unilines to form the New Zealand/Papua New Guinea Express service, which rationalised the sailings of the *Capitaine La Perouse*, *Capitaine Tasman* and *Forum Papua New Guinea*. This represented a reduction in overall tonnage because PFL had sold and not replaced the *Forum New Zealand II*.[249]

Her sale was a sad event for PFL yet reflected the need for a greater cashflow to help pay off the *Forum Papua New Guinea*. It also emphasised the absence of projected growth in freight volumes on the Papua New Guinea service.

In 1993 PFL again allied itself with Sofrana in the Australia–Fiji trade in a new venture called the Pacific Express Line which channelled PFL and Sofrana freight together. The new line continued for only two years but it signified a wider strategy to seek co-operation with other companies. John MacLennan observed in August 1995:

At this stage I see PFL tending increasingly towards a hubbing operation feeding out into the Pacific. In such a structure we will increasingly align ourselves with several major players.[250]

Shareholders have proved most reluctant to adopt Price Waterhouse recommendations in the matter of governance. There has been a general acceptance that the Memorandum of Understanding should be changed to allow for the freer trading of shares, although this has yet to be actioned. Shareholding countries were reluctant to remove the link with the Regional Shipping Council, in part because of its policy-setting role and further because it was a tangible link with the Forum. Most shareholders were reluctant to give up their powers to appoint directors and, while there was some agreement on the need to increase the skills on the board, it was felt that there must be other ways of achieving this. In the interim it was decided that all future appointments should be vetted by the chairman to achieve a better balance of skills.[251]

There appeared to be a willingness to place the Forum Line under some form of continuous audit as laid down by the newly developed strategic plan.[252] It is also possible that the shareholders' current favourable attitude towards maintaining their shares may change when PFL further improves its profitability. International experience suggests that there is more incentive to sell a state-owned (in this case regionally-owned) asset when it is in a viable condition.

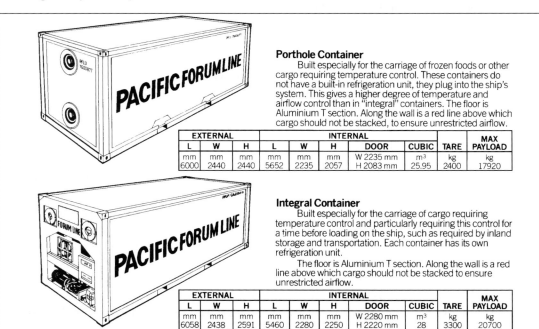

Porthole Container
 Built especially for the carriage of frozen foods or other cargo requiring temperature control. These containers do not have a built-in refrigeration unit, they plug into the ship's system. This gives a higher degree of temperature and airflow control than in "integral" containers. The floor is Aluminium T section. Along the wall is a red line above which cargo should not be stacked, to ensure unrestricted airflow.

EXTERNAL			INTERNAL						MAX
L	W	H	L	W	H	DOOR	CUBIC	TARE	PAYLOAD
mm	mm	mm	mm	mm	mm	W 2235 mm	m³	kg	kg
6000	2440	2440	5652	2235	2057	H 2083 mm	25.95	2400	17920

Integral Container
 Built especially for the carriage of cargo requiring temperature control and particularly requiring this control for a time before loading on the ship, such as required by inland storage and transportation. Each container has its own refrigeration unit.
 The floor is Aluminium T section. Along the wall is a red line above which cargo should not be stacked to ensure unrestricted airflow.

EXTERNAL			INTERNAL						MAX
L	W	H	L	W	H	DOOR	CUBIC	TARE	PAYLOAD
mm	mm	mm	mm	mm	mm	W 2280 mm	m³	kg	kg
6058	2438	2591	5460	2280	2250	H 2220 mm	28	3300	20700

Trans-Tasman Trade

As a result of the mounting losses, PFL management was by mid-1992 seeking ways to reduce overheads and improve revenue. An obvious solution was to cease employing expensive crews on the trans-Tasman route. Management estimated that having to man with New Zealanders cost PFL about NZ$1 million more than an international crew.[253]

At the same time PFL had insufficient space to service the Fiji trade. As the problem grew, management considered switching vessels so that the smaller ships with Island crews were on the trans-Tasman and the larger vessels on the South Pacific routes. It was envisaged that the move would not involve job losses for New Zealand seamen, but it would mean introducing Pacific Island crews into the Tasman, which would undermine the Trans-Tasman Accord.

Seamen's Union president Dave Morgan had been consulted and responded that he would rather have no service operating to Brisbane than have New Zealanders replaced by Pacific Islanders. Peter Kiely, the New Zealand director, was well aware of the potential industrial implications of switching the vessels but also very concerned at PFL's immediate plight. He observed in December 1992:

> The commercial decision seems clear to me. Either the Line must have the right to manage its own interests or we might as well place the whole management of the Line in the hands of Mr. Morgan.[254]

The suggestion to switch vessels was seriously contemplated and shareholders were canvassed. However, the Island directors were opposed to any move to take on the New Zealand maritime unions, while management were not keen on yet again being at the centre of a political controversy. It was decided to sell assets, which meant selling *Forum New Zealand II* to cut the loss on its service and to fund the debt on the *Forum Papua New Guinea*.[255]

The sale occurred at the same time as PFL's withdrawal from trans-Tasman trade. PFL's last link with this service was as agent for ANL via its joint FAST agencies. In mid-December 1996 ANL also announced the withdrawal of its trans-Tasman service, and FAST had suddenly to retrench. However, it had achieved sufficient brand recognition that PFL retained the name even after ANL sold what remained of its interest in the venture.[256]

The savings resulting from selling the *Forum New Zealand II* and withdrawing from Australian trade were still insufficient to restore the Papua New Guinea trade to profitability. PFL therefore sought an accommodation with Sofrana which was reinforced early in 1995 when PFL sold its second vessel, the *Forum Papua New Guinea*. As Sofrana and PFL had both operated one vessel on the run, PFL short-term chartered a Russian-registered ship, the *Socofl Stream*.

It was believed that with her international crew she would provide considerable savings. It meant also that, for the first time, PFL were operating without a New Zealand crew. This would previously have engendered industrial unrest but the climate had changed so dramatically in the preceding five years that the Seamen's Union was focussing its attention on the trans-Tasman trade, and PFL's move went largely unnoticed. However, the *Socofl Stream* proved unsatisfactory and costly. With PFL wishing to end her charter and Sofrana looking to develop its Papua New Guinea service alone, the joint PFL/Sofrana service ended.

The Forum Line still had a considerable presence in Papua New Guinea and was unwilling to abandon this. To Sofrana's surprise, PFL management arranged with Chief Container Services (Swires) for a fifteen-day New Zealand–Papua New Guinea service which was a mixture of direct CCS calls to Auckland and trans-shipment connections through Brisbane. CCS expansion into a New Zealand service was a considerable innovation. This began in May 1996 and proved profitable,[257] although PFL remained keen to re-establish its own vessel on the route.

Strong support for the Papua New Guinea service led PFL to upgrade its tonnage early in 1998 by slot chartering with its CCS partner in the *Coral Chief*. Marketing manager Ewan Grant was positive about the relationship with CCS: 'It has helped us achieve cost savings while improving operational efficiency and maintaining a strong presence in the market.' The *Coral Chief* is a 726-TEU capacity vessel which links Lyttelton, Napier, Auckland and Tauranga with Port Moresby, Lae and Rabaul. She has break-bulk capacity and carries her own lifting gear.[258]

PFL's short-term charter of the Russian Socofl Stream *to replace* Forum Papua New Guinea *meant employing an international crew for the first time.*

Above: PFL ended its joint Papua New Guinea service with Sofrana in 1996 and began to slot charter on Swires' Coral Chief.
Below: PFL and the Cook Islands National Line established a joint service to the Cooks in 1995 using the Thor Lisbeth.

Two New Services

PFL has developed a purely commercial service, in conjunction with the Cook Islands National Line, to Rarotonga and a New Zealand government aid service to the Tokelaus.

New Zealand subsidies for the joint Cook Island–Niue service had been phased out in 1987 and private competition encouraged. The Cook Islands National Line ran the *Ngarimu III* on a triangular route from Rarotonga to Napier and the Chatham Islands. The Napier link reflected an historical connection: there were more than 6000 Cook Islanders in Hawkes Bay.[259] PFL was unable to compete head-on with the Cook Islands National Line, as shipping to the Cooks was governed by a licensing system. Instead PFL offered a feeder service from Apia, where freight was trans-shipped to Rarotonga.[260]

At the close of the 1995 financial year PFL addressed the shortcomings of its Cook Islands service by entering into a joint service with the Cook Islands National Line. Translink had withdrawn its vessel and CINL was looking to pick up container business without too much risk, while PFL sought to improve its service and integrate it with other Pacific trades. PFL and the Cook Islands National Line chartered a small container vessel (the 85-TEU *Thor Lisbeth*) which was to service Auckland, Nuku'alofa, Apia and Rarotonga. The route was hurriedly set up to take advantage of a gap in the market. The Cook Islands service has proved profitable and the partnership with the Cook Islands National Line very productive.

While this service is strictly a commercial operation, the Tokelau service is a New Zealand aid project managed by PFL. Established in mid-1997, it runs between the Tokelaus and Samoa using the *Forum Tokelau*, a vessel acquired from the Cook Islands National Line.

Tokelau, with a population of only 3000, has no airport and only a limited communications system. It had previously relied almost exclusively on infrequent shipping services from Samoa. The PFL board recognised that under the Memorandum of Understanding it could have a role in providing services to the Tokelaus and discussed this with the Tokelau Local Authority and with New Zealand-based Tokelau administrator Lindsay Watt.

The Forum Line was anxious to avoid any open-ended arrangement, while the Tokelau Local Authority and New Zealand officials were keen that any subsidy should be explicit, transparent and financially efficient. Although there was a six-month delay in purchasing the vessel, the service has generally operated as envisaged. The Tokelau Local Authority sets freight and passenger charges and is provided with full information on the real costs of the service.

It was hoped that the current arrangements would be temporary and that, by the year 2000, Japan's overseas development budget would have provided a purpose-built vessel. In the meantime PFL fulfils its purpose by providing a necessary service while at the same time ensuring a return for shareholders.

Since there is still no significant air link, the Forum Tokelau service uses unitised passenger accommodation (a closer view below) designed by John MacLennan. This can be lifted off when the vessel carries only freight.

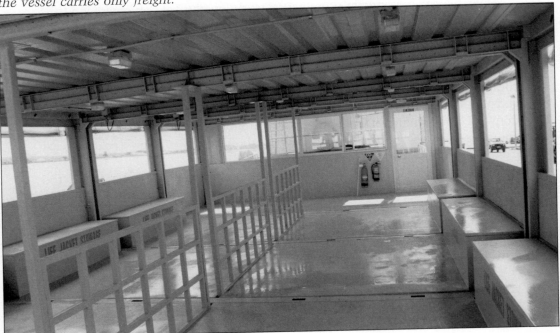

Conclusion

THE PACIFIC FORUM LINE is a unique blend of a commercial shipping venture and regional diplomacy whose name embodies its identity. It is wholly Pacific in its focus; it owes its origins to the regional spirit fostered from the time that the Pacific Islands became independent and it provides shipping services to Pacific ports. The line is a tangible expression of a unity of purpose among Pacific nations which has lasted for over twenty years and seems likely to continue. Ratu Sir Kamisese Mara was aware of the power of PFL as a symbol of wider Pacific co-operation when he observed that: 'You know symbolism is a great thing. When you see this boat floating around with the Forum symbol—it is a great thing.'

If the Forum Line is a single corporate entity, the shareholder states are diverse in terms of their size, population, ethnic origins and economic development. Despite differing shipping requirements, they recognise that in combining they can achieve goals not possible individually.

The Pacific Forum Line was very much a product of the drive for national and regional identity that emerged in the Pacific in the 1960s and has found enduring political expression in the South Pacific Forum. The line not only embodied regional aspirations but also shared the commercial risk that ship chartering and purchase posed for newly independent Island states, and gave the region's leaders an unprecedented degree of control over it. Through such co-operation, Forum governments were able to negotiate with the powerful New Zealand and Australian maritime unions and have Pacific Island crews on vessels trading in the region.

The Forum Line was naively established with virtually no capital, largely to facilitate participation by all Island states. It struggled from a position of weakness and had to compete vigorously to gain market share. This made it vulnerable to competition and locked it into unsuccessful commercial strategies designed for short-term survival. The struggle to fund losses dominated much of the Forum's agenda for nearly a decade and became the focus of tensions between New Zealand and Australia.

Perhaps more than any other issue, PFL funding rivalry demonstrated New Zealand's geographical identification with the Pacific and Australia's status as a medium-sized world power. Both countries may be accused of following self-interest in their attitude to PFL. New Zealand adopted a hands-on approach which reinforced its links with the Pacific, whereas Australia stood back in a guardian role, reinforced by its greater provision of bilateral aid.

The New Zealand government's response was pragmatic, backed by taxpayer funds. Such a strategy would be unlikely to be adopted by modern administrations confined by the Fiscal Responsibility Act. Recent governments have tended to judge the success or failure of any commercial operation by the size of its return on capital.

However, any such retrospective assessment of PFL in its early years would be anachronistic. In terms of its purposes in the Memorandum of Understanding—to recognise the strategic importance of shipping to the region, provide regular services, contain freight rates and establish strong rationalised shipping services between Island states—it was an almost unqualified success. It also met all but one of the six 'principal' objectives, including providing shipping services to cater for the special circumstances of the region. Its failing was that in its first eight years PFL was not profitable. However, the way in which the Forum rose to meet those losses was practical and carried out on the basis of a consensus which allowed vigorous debate even when this spilled over into the public arena.

The Pacific Forum Line's second decade has been relatively free from political controversy but the operation has had to wrestle with a highly competitive and rapidly changing industry. Profits, although hard to find, have finally been achieved and directors have approved the first dividend payment. Looking forward to the 21st century, they have adopted strategies which put the return on shareholders' funds at the forefront of the Forum Line's agenda.

In December 1997 the Governor-General of New Zealand, the Right Honourable Sir Michael Hardie Boys, hosted a function to commemorate the twentieth anniversary of the Pacific Forum Line. He is shown here with New Zealand Minister of Foreign Affairs, the Right Honourable Don McKinnon, and PFL executives.

Front row, left to right: Rt Hon. Don McKinnon, Mr T. H. Tufui (PFL Chairman), Rt Hon. Sir Michael Hardie Boys, Mr P. T. Kiely (New Zealand), Mr M. Tamarua (Papua New Guinea).

Back row, left to right: Mr W. J. MacLennan (Chief Executive PFL), Mr A. Vocea (Fiji), Mr M. Bradshaw (Nauru), Mr P. Hauia (Solomon Islands), Mr P. Fepulea'i (Samoa).

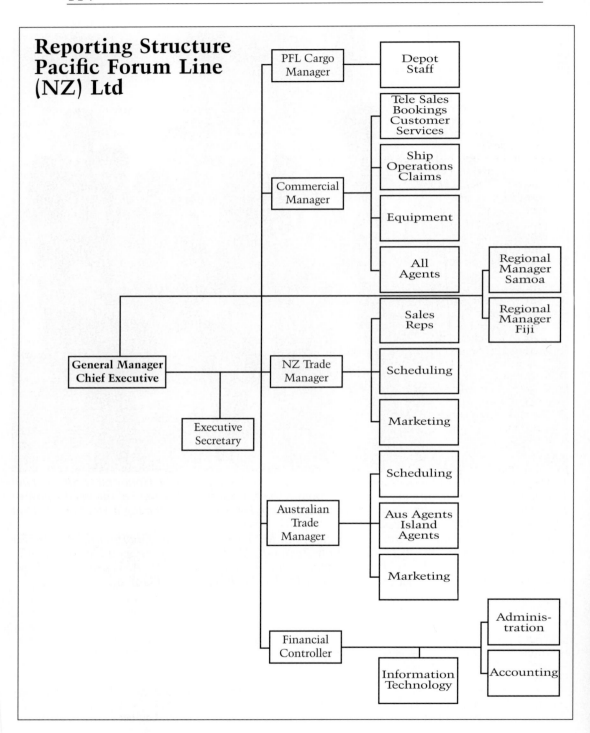

Reporting Structure Pacific Forum Line (NZ) Ltd

Notes

Introduction

1. Steve Hoadley, *The South Pacific Foreign Affairs Handbook* (Sydney, 1992), pp.18–19.
2. Tokelau does not fit the necessary UN conditions to be a territory or a self-governing state. For a discussion of its status see *The New Zealand Official Yearbook 1997*, p.96.
3. Steve Hoadley, *The South Pacific Foreign Affairs Handbook*, p.21.
4. This was true of post-war independence although Samoan protests at New Zealand administration, particularly in the late 1920s, were harshly put down. See Michael Field, *Mau: Samoa's Struggle Against New Zealand Oppression* (Wellington, 1984).
5. Ministry of Foreign Affairs, *South Pacific: Trade and Economic Prospects* (1994), pp.39–45.
6. Interview with His Excellency Ratu Sir Kamisese Mara, 2 March 1998.
7. Report of the South Pacific Policy Review Group, 'Towards a Pacific Island Community' (Wellington, 1990), pp.62–63.
8. Hoadley, *South Pacific Foreign Affairs Handbook*, pp.18, 24, 64.
9. Pacific Forum Line, 'Our Pacific: Our Shipping Line' inside cover, current promotional foldout.

Chapter 1

10. Union Steam Ship was sold to P&O in 1917. See Gavin McLean, *The Southern Octopus: The Rise of a Shipping Empire* (Wellington, 1990), and Gordon McLauchlan, *The Line That Dared: A History of the Union Steam Ship Company 1875–1975* (Auckland, 1987).
11. NZ National Archives, PM 36/2/16/1 part 2, Inwards Savingsgram, Australian High Commissioner, Suva, to Secretary Foreign Affairs, 30 June 1971.
12. Bryce Fraser (ed.), *The New Zealand Book of Events* (Auckland, 1986), p.88.
13. *ibid.*, p.92, and Gordon McLauchlan, *The Line That Dared*, Chapter 11.
14. Interview with Harry Julian, 12 December 1997.
15. Bryce Fraser (ed.), *The New Zealand Book of Events*, p.185.
16. *AJHR*, 1971, H-52, Report of the Commission of Inquiry into New Zealand Shipping, p.17.
17. National Archives, (Ministry of Foreign Affairs and Trade), PM 36/2/16/1 part 4, South Pacific Forum, Canberra, February 1972, 'Brief New Zealand Delegation'.
18. John R. Baker, 'Law and Development in Melanesia: Government Regulation of Ocean Liner Services in the Pacific Islands', (Seventh Waigani Seminar 2 May 1973) in National Archives, (Ministry of Foreign Affairs and Trade), PM 36/12/16/1 part 5.
19. Material from correspondence with George Fulcher, 10 March 1998.
20. Robert Gardiner and Alistair Cooper (eds.), *The Shipping Revolution: The Modern Merchant Ship* (Conways History of the Ship, London, 1992), pp.42–43.
21. Barry Pemberton, *Australian Coastal Shipping* (Melbourne University Press, 1979), p.221.
22. *AJHR*, 1971, H-52, Report of the Commission of Inquiry into New Zealand Shipping, pp.15–17.
23. John R. Baker, 'Law and Development in Melanesia: Government Regulation of Ocean Liner Services in the Pacific Islands'.
24. *Pacific Islands Monthly*, June 1975, p.85.
25. National Archives, (Ministry of Foreign Affairs and Trade), PM 36/2/161, part 2, Inwards Savingsgram, Australian High Commissioner, Suva, to Secretary Foreign Affairs, 30 June 1971.
26. John R. Baker, 'Law and Development in Melanesia', p.31.
27. *ibid.*, pp.15–16.
28. National Archives, (Ministry of Foreign Affairs and Trade), PM 36/2/16/1 part 5, File Note 'Cook Islands Viewpoint', 25/1/73.
29. *ibid.*, part 6, J. R. Springfield, Department of Maori and Island Affairs, to Secretary Foreign Affairs, 13 June 1973.
30. Correspondence with Harry Julian, 19 February 1998, and interview, 12 December 1997. Cook Islanders held New Zealand citizenship and the vessel was not cross-trading.
31. National Archives, (Ministry of Foreign Affairs and Trade), PM 36/2/16/1 part 3a, Report of Working Party on Pacific Island Shipping, 10 December 1971, p.44. The predecessor to the *Lorena*, the *Thallo*, had been crewed by Pacific

Islanders, but the company was forced to accept a New Zealand crew on the *Lorena*. Interview with Harry Julian, 12 December 1997.

32. *Evening Post*, 13 December 1971; National Archives, (Ministry of Foreign Affairs and Trade), PM 36/2/16/1 part 3a, Conversation Rt Hon. J. R. Marshall and Tupuola Efi, 5 June 1972.

33. National Archives, (Ministry of Foreign Affairs and Trade), PM 36/2/16/1 part 5, Briefing for PM's Visit to Cook Islands, April 1973.

34. *ibid.*, part 8, High Commissioner to Secretary Foreign Affairs, 21 March 1974; National Archives, (Ministry of Foreign Affairs and Trade), PM 36/2/16/1 part 5, Report on PM's visit to Cook Islands, April 1973, Secretary Foreign Affairs to PM Cook Island Shipping Service, 19 October 1973, Minister of Mines and Immigration Fraser Colman to Prime Minister, 7 November 1973.

35. *ibid.*, part 3a, Quoted in Officials Advisory Committee on Overseas Shipping: Report of the Working Party on Island Shipping, 10 December 1971, p.53.

36. *ibid.*, p.39. See Conrad Bollinger, *Against the Wind: The Story of the New Zealand Seamen's Union* (Wellington, New Zealand Seamen's Union, 1968), p.179.

37. *The Press*, 8 September 1971.

38. National Archives, (Ministry of Foreign Affairs and Trade), PM 36/2/16/1 part 5, His Excellency President Hammer DeRoburt of Nauru to Sir Basil Arthur, Minister of Transport, 31 May 1973.

39. *ibid.*, E. G. Davey, Secretary of Labour, to Minister of Labour, 22 June 1973.

40. *National Business Review*, vol. 3, No. 19 (23 July 1973), p.1.

41. National Archives, (Ministry of Foreign Affairs and Trade), PM 36/2/16/1 part 7, Frank Corner, Secretary Foreign Affairs, to Prime Minister, 1 September 1973.

42. *ibid.*, part 6, Toby Hill, President of the Combined Maritime Unions, and Secretary K. Douglas, to Secretary of Labour, 13 August 1973.

43. *ibid.*, Secretary Foreign Affairs to Secretaries of Transport, Trade and Industry, Labour, Maori and Island Affairs, 'New Zealand/Pacific Island Shipping Conference', 26 September 1973

44. *ibid.*, Draft Telegram Wellington—High Commissioners in Apia, Suva and Canberra—undated but *c.* 13 July 1973.

45. *ibid.*, High Commission Canberra to Secretary Foreign Affairs, 3 August 1973.

46. *ibid.*, part 7, Text of Address of Prime Minister of New Zealand, the Rt Hon. N. E. Kirk, at the opening of the New Zealand/Pacific Islands Shipping Conference at Waitangi Hotel, Waitangi on Thursday 25 October 1973 at 10.30 am.

47. As a shipowner Harry Julian opposed the formation of any government-owned shipping line, including PFL, at the time of its formation in 1978. Interview with Harry Julian, 12 December 1997.

48. National Archives, (Ministry of Foreign Affairs and Trade), PM 36/2/16/1 part 7, Sent in diplomatic bag from Honiara, copy of letter D. E. Gleason, Pacific Island Territories Department (UK) to T. Russel Esq. CBE, Honiara, 21 September 1973.

49. *ibid.*, New Zealand/Pacific Islands Shipping Conference Waitangi, 25–27 October 1973, Joint Communiqué.

50. *ibid.*, *Tonga Chronicle*, 8 November 1973, report by Bob McLelland of Auckland.

51. *ibid.*

52. *ibid.*, Telex High Commission to Secretary Foreign Affairs, 17 December 1973, and Wellington to High Commission Canberra, 20 December 1973. See also National Archives, (Ministry of Foreign Affairs and Trade), PM 36/2/16/1 part 9, Secretary of Labour to Secretary Foreign Affairs, 9 May 1974.

53. *ibid.*, part 2, *Fiji Times* cutting, 15 September 1971.

54. *ibid.*, part 5, File Note 'South Pacific Shipping: Tarros Proposals', undated but *c.* 6 March 1973.

55. *ibid.*, Note for File 'Shipping Union TNT Services', 27 November 1972.

56. *ibid.*, High Commission Suva to Wellington, Telex, 6 December 1972.

57. *ibid.*, part 3, Seminar on Shipping in the South West Pacific.

58. *ibid.*, part 5, File Note 'Tonga: Tarros Shipping Proposal', 1 March 1973.

59. *ibid.*, South Pacific Forum, Apia, 17–19 April 1973, New Zealand Briefing Paper.

60. *ibid.*, part 7, Notes of a Meeting held at 9.00 am on 30 October 1973 with Mr. K. W. Piddington, Deputy Director SPEC, on South Pacific Shipping.

61. *ibid.*, part 2, Press Communiqué from PIPA Conference held at Nuku'alofa, 31 August–2 September 1971.

62. *ibid.*, part 3a, Officials Advisory Committee on Overseas Shipping: Report of Working Party on Pacific Island Shipping, 10 December 1971, pp.16–21.

63. *ibid.*, p.30.

64. NZ National Archives, ABHS 950, 301/14/13 part 27, Statement in Canberra by Mr Middleton, 'Development of a Regional Shipping Line in the South Pacific', April 1982.

65. National Archives, (Ministry of Foreign Affairs and Trade), PM 36/2/16/1 part 3a, Officials Advisory Committee on Overseas Shipping, p.37.

66. *ibid.*, part 3, Seminar on Shipping in the South Pacific, 30 August –1 September 1972, 'Agreed Resumé'.

67. *ibid.*, part 3, 'Report of the New Zealand Delegates'.

68. *ibid.*, part 4, Report by Cooper Brothers and Co., R. S. Kay and Co., Chartered Accountants, Suva, on Accounting Study of the Tonga Shipping Agency (now the Pacific Navigation Company), p.3.

69. *ibid.*, part 3, Seminar on Shipping in the South Pacific, 30 August –1 September 1972, 'Report of the New Zealand Delegates', p.7.

70. *ibid.*, part 7, Mahe Tupouniua, address to Waitangi Conference, 25–27 October 1973.

71. *ibid.*, part 7, Secretary Foreign Affairs to Secretary Transport, 26 September 1973.

72. Australian Archives, Department of Foreign Affairs and Trade, A 1838/1, (278/5/1), part 3, R. H. Robertson, First Assistant Secretary Western Division, to the Minister of Foreign Affairs, 'Regional Shipping', 3 June 1975, and Department Foreign Affairs/Department of Trade, 'Proposed Shipping Line: Background for Meeting with New Zealand Prime Minister Rowling', 13 March 1975.

73. *ibid.*, 'Draft Brief for the Australian Delegation to the South Pacific Regional Shipping Advisory Board Meeting, 2–3 June, 1975, Suva and the Council Meeting, 6–7 June, 1975 Suva'.

74. *ibid.*, Maris King, Acting High Commissioner Suva, to Secretary Department Foreign Affairs, 'South Pacific Regional Shipping', 5 March 1975.

75. Interview with Francis Hong Tiy, 3 March 1998.

76. NZ National Archives, ABHS 950, 301/14/13 part 27, Statement in Canberra by Mr Middleton, 'Development of a Regional Shipping Line in the South Pacific', April 1982, p.9. Note: much of this overview of the formal process of the establishment of the line stems from this document, but it is supplemented with detail from elsewhere.

Chapter 2

77. NZ National Archives, Transport (Tr), W2929, 2/7/92/2, vol. 3, Officials Committee on Transport Report to the Minister of Transport, 'South Pacific Regional Shipping Line', 3 February 1976.

78. Australian Archives, Department of Foreign Affairs, A 1838/1 (278/5/1), part 6, Australian High Commissioner Nauru to Miss M. King, Australian High Commission, Suva, 21 June 1976, and P. J. Nixon, Minister of Transport, to A. S. Peacock, Minister of Foreign Affairs, 31 May 1976.

79. *ibid.*, Australian High Commissioner Nauru to Miss M. King, Australian High Commission, Suva, 21 June 1976.

80. NZ National Archives, Transport (Tr), W2929, 2/7/92/2, vol. 3, Officials Committee on Transport Report to the Minister of Transport, 'South Pacific Regional Shipping Line', 3 February 1976.

81. *ibid.*, and interview with Rod Gates, 11 December 1997.

82. NZ National Archives, ABHS 950, 301/14/13, part 9, Precis of the Articles of the Memorandum of Understanding, *c.* May 1977.

83. *ibid.*, part 5, 'South Pacific Forum: Nauru: 26–28 July 1976. Summary Record'.

84. *ibid.*

85. *Dominion*, 11 May 1977.

86. *Evening Post*, 11 May 1977.

87. NZ National Archives, (Tr), W2929, 2/7/92/2, vol. 3, Memo, Secretary for Transport to Minister of Transport, 19 February 1976, 'The New Zealand Maritime Unions and the Proposed Pacific Forum Line', pp.2–5.

88. NZ National Archives, ABHS 950, 301/14/13, part 6, Draft Memo, 18 August 1976, 'Visit of Parliamentary Delegation South Pacific Shipping'.

89. *ibid.*, part 12, General Background Notes PFL *c.* June 1977, and *National Business Review*, 7 June 1978.

Pages 32–45

90. *ibid.*, part 12, Minutes of Officials Sub-Committee on Transport held Aurora House, Room 830, 9.00 am, 1 March 1978, and Secretary of Transport to Minister of Transport, 7 March 1978.

91. *ibid.*, part 9, NZ Ambassador Bonn to Secretary Foreign Affairs, 23 November 1977.

92. *ibid.*, NZ Ambassador Bonn to Secretary Foreign Affairs, 23 November 1977. For a detailed breakdown of the agreements see ABHS 950, 301/14/13 part 13, NZ Ambassador Bonn to Secretary Foreign Affairs, 'South Pacific Shipping: German Aid to Tonga and Samoa', 27 July 1978.

93. *ibid.*, part 11, Officials Working Party, Sub-Committee on Transport 'A Survey of New Zealand/South Pacific Services', December 1977, NZ/Tonga section.

94. *ibid.*, part 9, Ambassador Bonn to Secretary Foreign Affairs, 14 December 1977.

95. *ibid.*, part 13, Memorandum Dr K. Uphoff, Columbus Line Hamburg, to Hon. Edia Olevale, Minister of Foreign Affairs and Trade, Papua New Guinea, 22 March 1978. Uphoff describes Columbus's Pacific trade and development in some detail in response to Papua New Guinea's rejection of what they saw as 'tied' aid.

96. Bryce Taylor (ed.), *The New Zealand Book of Events*, p.92.

97. NZ National Archives, ABHS 950, 301/14/13 part 11, New Zealand Officials Working Party, 'A Survey of New Zealand/South Pacific Shipping Services, December 1977'.

98. *ibid.*, part 13, Pacific Forum Line: Ratification Received as at 20 July 1978.

99. *ibid.*, Chairman's Report to the Shareholders of the Pacific Forum Line Ltd, 19 June 1978.

100. *ibid.*, part 13, Minutes of the First Meeting of the Board of Directors of the Pacific Forum Line held in Apia, Samoa on 26 July 1977.

101. *Business News*, July 1980, p.7.

102. NZ National Archives, ABHS 950, 301/14/13 part 13, Secretary Foreign Affairs to Pacific High Commissioners and High Commissioner London, and Ambassadors to Bonn and Washington, 'Pacific Forum Line', 12 October 1978, and 301/14/13 part 15, *Pacific Newsletter*, 'Interview with Gordon Dewsnap', 24 February 1979.

103. *ibid.*, part 12, Background Notes for Officials Sub-Committee on Transport Meeting 9.30 am, Wed., 1 March 1978, Room 830, Aurora House.

104. *New Zealand Herald*, 3 March 1978.

105. *ibid.*

106. NZ National Archives, ABHS 950, 301/14/13 part 13, High Commissioner Nuku'alofa to Secretary Foreign Affairs, 25 August 1978.

107. *ibid.*, Secretary Foreign Affairs to Pacific High Commissioners and High Commissioner London, and Ambassadors to Bonn and Washington, 'Pacific Forum Line', 12 October 1978.

108. *ibid.*, part 14, Pacific Forum Line Officials Meeting, 12–13 February 1979, Auckland, pp.2–3.

109. *ibid.*, part 13, Attachment to Report of SPEC Committee Meeting, Niue, 11–15 September 1978.

110. *ibid.*, PFL: Staff and Building Report, 28 September 1978.

111. *ibid.*, part 14, Ninth South Pacific Forum: Niue: 15–22 September 1978: Regional Shipping.

112. *ibid.*, Record of Discussion with General Manager, PFL, Mr Gordon Dewsnap, at Meeting of Officials Sub-Committee on Transport, 13 November 1978.

113. *ibid.*, part 16, SPEC Committee Meeting, 5–6 July 1979, Honiara.

114. *ibid.*, part 14, Record of Discussion with General Manager, PFL, Mr Gordon Dewsnap, at Meeting of Officials Sub-Committee on Transport, 13 November 1978.

115. *ibid.*, SPEC Committee: Budget Meeting: Agenda Item 7(d): Pacific Forum Line.

116. *ibid.*, part 15, Minister of Transport, Memo for Cabinet Economic Committee, associated with E (79)M3 part III, 7 February 1979.

117. *ibid.*, part 16, Memo G. K. Ward, Pacific Division, to Messrs Cotton, Stewart and Templeton, undated but *c.* 19 May 1979.

118. *ibid.*, part 15 Minister of Transport; Memo for Cabinet Economic Committee, associated with E (79) M3 part III, 7 February 1979.

119. *ibid.*, part 16, South Pacific Regional Shipping Council: Pacific Forum Line, 19 July 1979, pp.1–10.

120. Australian Archives, Department of Foreign Affairs, A 1838/1 (278/5/1) part 17, Record of the IDC Meeting on the Consultant's Report on a Future Plan for the Pacific Forum Line, 12 July 1979, Mr Cole, p.1.

121. *ibid.*, Inward Cablegram High Commissioner Wellington to Canberra, 12 July 1979.

Pages 46–58

122. NZ National Archives, ABHS 950, 301/14/13 part 17, Cabinet Economic Committee Officials Paper, 'South Pacific Regional Shipping Council—Pacific Forum Line' (date obscured), August 1979. See also part 16, 2YA Morning Report 2 August 1979 for an overview of the public reporting of the meeting.
123. *ibid.*, part 17, High Commissioner to Secretary Foreign Affairs and Other Pacific Posts, 6 August 1979.
124. *Business News*, July 1980, pp.5–8.
125. NZ National Archives, ABHS 950, 301/14/13 part 17, Briefing on Mt Hagen Papua New Guinea Meeting 'Pacific Forum Line', 5 September 1979.
126. *ibid.*, part 17, Wellington to High Commissioner Apia, 1 December 1979.

Chapter 3

127. *ibid.*, part 18, Telex, High Commission Apia to Secretary Foreign Affairs, Wellington, 25 February 1980.
128. *ibid.*, and *Samoa Times*, 7 and 14 November 1980.
129. *Business News*, July 1980, Felise Va'a, 'The PFL Dilemma: Service or Profitability'.
130. *ibid.*
131. *National Business Review*, 6 October 1980, pp.26–27.
132. NZ National Archives, ABHS 950, 301/14/13 part 10, *Tonga Chronicle*, 16 September 1976.
133. *ibid.*, part 19, Secretary of Transport to Minister of Transport, 'Pacific Forum Line: Finances', 11 June 1980.
134. Correspondence with George Fulcher, 10 March 1998.
135. NZ National Archives, ABHS 950, 301/14/13 part 20, Cabinet Economic Committee Paper, 'South Pacific Regional Shipping Council: The Future of the Pacific Forum Line', 15 August 1980.
136. *ibid.*, part 21, Telex High Commission Canberra to Secretary Foreign Affairs Wellington, 19 August 1980.
137. The ramps when installed were some of the largest of their kind. There was considerable controversy at the time as to the suitability of the two West German vessels. It seems clear that PFL had limited input into the vessel design, but the controversy disappeared after the line became profitable.
138. NZ National Archives, ABHS 950, 301/14/13 part 20, Cabinet Economic Committee 'South Pacific Regional Shipping Council: The Future of the Pacific Forum Line', 15 August 1980, earlier drafts of same paper, and draft 'Pacific Forum Line (PFL) Background'.
139. *ibid.*, part 21, Briefing CHOGM, Delhi, 4–8 September 1980, Mini Forum, 'PFL'.
140. *ibid.*
141. *ibid.*
142. *ibid.*, Telex High Commissioner Canberra to Secretary Foreign Affairs Wellington, 8 September 1980.
143. *ibid.*, Telex (Secret) From Muldoon Delhi to Talboys Wellington, 8 September 1980. The telegram account matches very closely Muldoon's comments in Robert Muldoon, *My Way* (Auckland, A. H. and A. W. Reed, 1981), pp.152–3.
144. *ibid.*, part 22, Draft Report, p.1, 2 February 1981.
145. *ibid.*, part 21, Erwin Ludewig (Hamburg Süd), to Hon. Tupuola Efi, 8 October 1980.
146. *ibid.*, D. W. Young, Permanent Head of PM's Department to PM, 'PFL: Draft Report by Consultants', 2 February 1981.
147. Harry Julian doubted the value of Touche Ross exercise and saw many of the recommendations as a reflection of what management and the board were already doing. Interview with Harry Julian, 12 December 1997, and correspondence, 22 February 1998.
148. NZ National Archives, ABHS 950, 301/14/13 part 26, Minister of Transport, Memorandum for Cabinet, undated but early October 1981.
149. Interview with Harry Julian, 12 December 1997.
150. NZ National Archives, ABHS 950, 301/14/13 part 25a, Telex Consultants to Director SPEC, 4 August 1981.
151. *ibid.*
152. *ibid.*, part 21, R. P. Shea to SPEC Director Dr G. Gris, 10 October 1980.
153. *ibid.*, Cabinet Office Memo for Minister of Transport, 10 November 1980.
154. *National Business Review*, 24 November 1980.
155. *ibid.*, 8 December 1980, p.1.
156. NZ National Archives, ABHS 950, 301/14/13 part 25, Morning Report, Transcript of interview with Harry Julian, 2YA, 7.00 am, 2 March 1982.

Pages 59–72

157. *ibid.*, part 23, Transcript Morning Report 2YA, 7.00 am, 7 April 1981.
158. *ibid.*, part 23, Robert Muldoon Press Conference Notes, *c.* 7 April 1981.
159. *The Fiji Times*, Rt Hon. Ratu Sir Kamisese Mara, 'Fiji and the Pacific Forum Line', 2 May 1981.
160. NZ National Archives, ABHS 950, 301/14/13 part 23. See commentary letter attached to article as well as Rt Hon. Ratu Sir Kamisese Mara, 'Fiji and the Pacific Forum Line', *The Fiji Times*, 2 May 1981.
161. *The Fiji Times*, Rt Hon. Ratu Sir Kamisese Mara, 'Fiji and the Pacific Forum Line', 2 May 1981.
162. Interview with Harry Julian, 12 December 1997.
163. Interview with His Excellency Ratu Sir Kamisese Mara, 2 March 1998.
164. NZ National Archives, ABHS 950, 301/14/13 part 24, Secretary Foreign Affairs to the Minister of Foreign Affairs, 'Pacific Forum Line', 19 August 1981.
165. *ibid.*, part 24, Memorandum for the Cabinet Economic Committee, 'Pacific Forum Line', undated but *c.* 19 August 1981.
166. *ibid.*, part 25, General Manager's Report, March 1982.
167. Pacific Forum Line: General Information Manual: History.
168. NZ National Archives, ABHS 950, 301/14/13 part 25, Draft CEC Paper, 'South Pacific Regional Shipping Council: The Future of the Pacific Forum Line', undated but end of March to early April 1982.
169. *ibid.*, part 30, 'Pacific Forum Line: Establishment History'.
170. *ibid.*, part 29, Secretary Foreign Affairs to Minister Foreign Affairs, 'Pacific Forum Line', 18 March 1983.
171. *ibid.*, part 34, Minister Foreign Affairs to Cabinet External Relations and Security Committee, 'Pacific Forum Line: Additional Funding Requirement', 17 August 1984. The New Zealand Cabinet decided to fund half of the additional losses in June 1983. This was first announced at the Regional Shipping Council in Honiara in June 1983 and reiterated at the Canberra Forum.
172. *ibid.*, part 31, D. P. Morris SPA Division to Messrs Shroff, Miller and Templeton, 'The Pacific Forum Line', 11 November 1983.

173. *ibid.*, part 30, D. P. Morris SPA Division to Messrs Shroff, Miller and Templeton, 'Pacific Forum Line: Record of Discussions in Auckland on 5 October 1983 with the PFL Management and the European Investment Bank', 11 October 1983, Telex, and High Commissioner Canberra to Secretary Foreign Affairs Wellington, 19 September 1983.
174. *ibid.*, part 30, 'Pacific Forum Line: Establishment History'.
175. *National Business Review*, 21 February 1983, p.22, and 28 February 1983, pp.3, 12.
176. NZ National Archives, ABHS 950, 301/14/13 part 30, Minutes of Meeting AIDAB officials and Harry Julian, 17 August 1983.
177. *Islands Business*, October 1983, 'Death Knell at the Forum', pp.21–22.
178. *ibid.*, p.22.
179. NZ National Archives, ABHS 950, 301/14/13 part 32, Papua New Guinea Press Release 1 March 1984, Radio Australia, News Summary, 24 April 1984, and *Post Courier*, 10 May 1984.
180. *ibid.*, parts 30–32, particularly part 32, I. C. Small to Mr S. Carlaw, Controller Maritime Policy MOT, 14 February 1984.
181. *ibid.*, part 34, Samoan government's official journal, *Savali*, 'PFL Disagreement to be Resolved at Tuvalu', 10 August 1984.
182. *ibid.*, part 33, 'Meeting with Mr Harry Julian', 12 June 1984.
183. *ibid.*, *The Evening Post*, 24 July 1984.
184. *ibid.*, part 34, Telex, High Commission to Secretary Foreign Affairs, Wellington, 13 August 1984.
185. *ibid.*, part 32, *National Business Review*, 23 April 1984.
186. *ibid.*, Transcript, Radio Australia news item, 29 May 1984.

Chapter 4

187. *ibid.*, part 34, Secretary Foreign Affairs to Minister Foreign Affairs, 'Pacific Forum Line: Additional Funding Requirement', 17 August 1984.
188. *ibid.*, Memo, H. Bremner (Trade and Industry) to DS (T), 15 August 1984.
189. *ibid.*, Extract from the Prime Minister's Post-Forum Press Conference, 28 August 1984, and widely reported in New Zealand newspapers.
190. *ibid.*, Telex, Suva High Commission to Wellington, 28 August 1984, relaying content of article, *Fiji Times*, 28 August 1984.

191. *ibid.*, Secretary Treasury to Minister of Finance, 'Pacific Forum Line: Overdraft Guarantee', 31 August 1984.

192. *ibid.*

193. The Labour-appointed New Zealand director says he was unaware of any political sympathy with the Treasury line. Interview with Michael Hirschfeld, 5 November 1997.

194. NZ National Archives, ABHS 950, 301/14/13 part 36, Pacific Forum Line: Officials Report 27 June 1985, Appendix D. N.B.: this the post-capitalisation shareholding of the main, Samoan company.

195. *ibid.*, part 41, Secretary Foreign Affairs and Trade to Minister of Transport, 'Visit by Mr Erwin Ludewig', 19 November 1986.

196. *ibid.*, part 43.

197. *ibid.*, B. A. Martin, 'PFL: Extraordinary General Meeting of Shareholders', 30 November 1987.

198. *ibid.*, part 36, PFL 'Proposal for Replacement of *Forum New Zealand*', 9 October 1986, pp.1–4.

199. *ibid.*, part 44, C.V. Bell for Secretary Foreign Affairs to Minister Foreign Affairs, 'Failure to Finalise Time Charter with New Zealand Line', 12 September 1988.

200. Ian Farquhar, *Jack of All Trades, Master of None: The Shipping Corporation of New Zealand 1973–1989* (Wellington, 1996), pp.30–32.

201. Gavin McLean, *Masters or Servants? A Short History of the New Zealand Merchant Service Guild* (Wellington, 1990), pp.75–79.

202. Interview with Dave Morgan, President of the New Zealand Seamen's Union, 13 October 1997.

203. Quoted in Ian Farquhar, *Jack of All Trades, Master of None*, p.33.

204. NZ National Archives, ABHS 950, 301/14/13 part 45, Oral Question, Mr B. Birch, 'Will the Minister of SOE review his decision to stop the sale of the *Weka* to PFL?', 28 February 1989.

205. *ibid.*, Telex, Secretary Foreign Affairs to Pacific Posts, 7 March 1989. A MERT press release on 14 April 1989 informed the public of the sale and crewing agreement.

206. *ibid.*, PFL Annual General Meeting of Shareholders, 17 August 1989.

207. Report From the Board of Directors of PFL Ltd to the Company Shareholders, April 1982, p.11.

208. Most of the chronology for this material comes from Pacific Forum Line, 'General Information Manual'.

Chapter 5

209. NZ National Archives, ABHS 950, 301/14/13, part 21, High Commissioner Suva to Secretary Foreign Affairs, 1 October 1980.

210. Report from the Board of Directors of Pacific Forum Line to the Company Shareholders, August 1980.

211. Report from the Board of Directors of Pacific Forum Line to the Company Shareholders, Cairns, June 1980.

212. Australian Archives, A 1838/1 (278/5/1), part 34, Program: Regional Shipping Line, 'Visit by Chairman of PFL (Mr Harry Julian)', 2 December 1981.

213. Interview with His Excellency Ratu Sir Kamisese Mara, 2 March 1998.

214. NZ National Archives, ABHS 950, 301/14/13 part 24, Secretary Foreign Affairs to Minister Foreign Affairs, 'Pacific Forum Line', 19 August 1981.

215. PFL, Head Office, 'Extraordinary Meeting of PFL Shareholders', March 1993.

216. NZ National Archives, ABHS 950, 301/14/13 part 24, Transcript, Morning Report (2YA), 7.00 am, 8 October 1981.

217. *ibid.*, part 33, Fifteenth South Pacific Forum: Tuvalu 27–28 August 1984, 'Pacific Forum Line: Progress Report'.

218. *ibid.*, part 38, N. F. Naisali, Minister of Finance, Tuvalu, to George Fulcher, PFL General Manager, 17 December 1985. See also High Commissioner Suva to Secretary Foreign Affairs, 10 January 1986.

219. *ibid.*, part 44, Feeder Service, Notes on Meeting in Suva with Secretaries to Governments of Kiribati and Tuvalu, 8 October 1988.

220. *ibid.*, part 37, G. C. Fortune for Secretary Foreign Affairs, S. S. Carlaw for Secretary for Transport and R. F. Shallcrass for Secretary to the Treasury to Ministers of Foreign Affairs, Finance and Transport, 'Pacific Forum Line: Feeder Service to Tuvalu and Kiribati', 18 December 1985.

221. *ibid.*, part 44, Feeder Service, Notes on Meeting in Suva with Secretaries to Governments of Kiribati and Tuvalu, 8 October 1988.

222. MOT File 2/7/92/1, part 4, Forum Secretariat, SPS(91)SPMDP.7, 'South Pacific Maritime

Pages 91–109

Development Programme Management Group, Fifth Meeting: Agenda Item 7: Lome III Maritime Project, 20 May 1991'.

223. Australian Archives, A 1838/1 (278/5/1), part 34, Program: Regional Shipping Line, 'Pacific Forum Line (PFL) — Extension of Feeder Services', 19 July 1985.

224. NZ National Archives, ABHS 950, 301/14/13 part 45, 'Brief Summary of the Regional Shipping Line's Performance since 1985'.

225. MOT File 2/7/92/1, part 4, Forum Secretariat, SPS(91)SPMDP.7, 'South Pacific Maritime Development Programme Management Group, Fifth Meeting: Agenda Item 7: Lome III Maritime Project, 20 May 1991'.

226. Report from the Pacific Forum Line Board of Directors to the Company Shareholders, September 1992.

227. High Commissioner Suva to Secretary Foreign Affairs, Wellington, 5 March 1993.

228. March 1993 Extraordinary Meeting of PFL Company Shareholders.

Chapter 6

229. NZ National Archives, ABHS 950, 301/14/13, part 47, Pacific Islands, Forum Secretariat, 'Regional Shipping, Shipping Regulatory and Policy Framework', 1 July 1997.

230. Report of the Pacific Forum Line Board of Directors to the Company Shareholders, 1989.

231. *New Zealand Shipping Gazette*, 3 March 1990, pp.7–8.

232. NZ National Archives, ABHS 950, 301/14/13, part 47, Pacific Islands, Forum Secretariat.

233. *New Zealand Shipping Gazette*, 19 May 1990, p.7.

234. Report of the Pacific Forum Line Board of Directors to the Company Shareholders, 1990, p.1.

235. *New Zealand Shipping Gazette*, 15 December 1990, pp.7–8.

236. Report of the Pacific Forum Line Board of Directors to the Company Shareholders, September 1993, p.1.

237. *ibid.*, 1991, p.37.

238. *ibid.*, 1992, pp.1–3.

239. *ibid.*, 1991, p.14.

240. *ibid.*, September 1993.

241. Price Waterhouse, Pacific Forum Line: Final Report, October 1994, p.31.

242. *ibid.*, p.27.

243. *ibid.*, pp.13–14.

244. *ibid.*, pp.9–10.

245. PFL began a service to the Cook Islands in 1995.

246. Price Waterhouse, Pacific Forum Line: Final Report, pp.1–5.

247. NZ National Archives, ABHS 950, 301/14/13, part 51, 'PFL Review's Final Report', 6 January 1995.

248. *New Zealand Shipping Gazette*, 5 September 1992, p.7.

249. *ibid.*, 17 July 1993, p.13.

250. *ibid.*, 5 August 1995, pp.1, 4.

251. Report of the Pacific Forum Line Board of Directors to the Company Shareholders, September 1995, and NZ National Archives, ABHS 950, 301/14/13, part 52, Telex High Commissioner Nuku'alofa to Secretary Foreign Affairs Wellington, 10 July 1995.

252. NZ National Archives, ABHS 950, 301/14/13, part 52, 'Crown Company Monitoring Advisory Unit', 7 June 1996.

253. *ibid.*, part 49, Pacific Islands, Forum Secretariat, Peter Kiely to Paul Cotton, NZ Consul General, Sydney, 16 April 1993.

254. *ibid.*, part 48, Pacific Islands, Forum Secretariat, Peter Kiely to Minister of Transport, 11 December 1992.

255. Conversation with Peter Kiely.

256. *New Zealand Shipping Gazette*, 30 November 1996, pp.7–9 (and Annual Report).

257. *New Zealand Shipping Gazette*, 26 April 1996, pp.7–8.

258. *ibid.*, 24 January 1998, pp.1, 4.

259. NZ National Archives, ABHS 950, 301/14/13, part 49: 'South Pacific Division: Background Notes, 27 July 1993'.

260. Report from the Board of Directors of PFL to the Company Shareholders, September 1990, p.22.

Bibliography

Primary Sources

(a) Reports

AJHR, 1971, H-52, Report of the Commission of Inquiry into New Zealand Shipping.

Pacific Forum Line, General Information Manual.

Pacific Forum Line, Our Pacific: Our Shipping Line (*c.* 1994).

Pacific Forum Line, Report From the Board of Directors of PFL Ltd. to the Company Shareholders, 1977–97.

Pacific Forum Line, Report of Extraordinary Meeting of PFL Company Shareholders, March 1993.

Price Waterhouse, Pacific Forum Line: Final Report, October 1994.

South Pacific Commission, South Pacific Economic and Social Statistics (SPESS) (various series beginning 1976).

Touche Ross, Report on Pacific Forum Line (Auckland, 1983).

(b) Files

Australian Archives:

Department of Foreign Affairs and Trade, A 1838/1, (278/5/1): Program: Regional Shipping Line, parts 1–44 (21 December 1972–4 November 1987).

New Zealand Archives:

National Archives, ABHS 950, 301/14/13: SPEC: Regional Shipping, parts 1–37 (May 1976–December 1985)

National Archives, (Ministry of Foreign Affairs and Trade), PM 36/2/16/1: Transport: Shipping, Shipping Services Between New Zealand and Pacific Islands General, parts 1–12 (September 1971–May 1979).

National Archives: Ministry of Transport, Series 1, W2929, 2/7/92, SPEC vol. 3, 1974–75.

National Archives: Ministry of Transport, Series 1, W2929, 2/7/92/1, SPEC vol. 1, 1974–76.

National Archives: Ministry of Transport, Series 1, W2929, 2/7/92/2, South Pacific Shipping Advisory Board, vols 2–4, 1975–76.

New Zealand Ministry of Foreign Affairs and Trade, File 301/14/13: South Pacific Forum Secretariat, Regional Shipping, parts 38–54 (December 1985–January 1998).

New Zealand Ministry of Transport, MOT File 2/7/92/1, part 4, South Pacific Regional Shipping Council, August 1985–July 1991.

New Zealand Ministry of Transport, MOT File 4/4/4 vol. 1 (now p 16120), Maritime International: Pacific Forum Line, March 1993–November 1993.

New Zealand Ministry of Transport, MOT File P5 /13, Pacific Forum Line, parts 1–2, December 1993–May 1996.

Secondary Sources

John R. Baker, 'Law and Development in Melanesia: Government Regulation of Ocean Liner Services in the Pacific Islands', (Seventh Waigani Seminar, 2 May 1973).

Conrad Bollinger, *Against the Wind: The Story of the New Zealand Seamen's Union* (Wellington, New Zealand Seamen's Union, 1968).

Ian Farquhar, *Jack of All Trades, Master of None: The Shipping Corporation of New Zealand 1973–1989* (Wellington, New Zealand Ship and Marine Society Inc.,1996).

Bryce Fraser (ed.), *The New Zealand Book of Events* (Auckland, Reed–Methuen, 1986).

Robert Gardiner and Alistair Couper (eds) 'The Shipping Revolution: The Modern Merchant Ship' (*Conway's History of the Ship*, London, Conway Maritime, 1992).

Steve Hoadley, *The South Pacific Foreign Affairs Handbook* (Sydney, Allen and Unwin in association with the New Zealand Institute of International Affairs, 1992).

Gordon McLauchlan, *The Line That Dared: A History of the Union Steam Ship Company 1875–1975* (Auckland, Four Star Books, 1987).

Gavin McLean, *Masters or Servants? A Short History of the New Zealand Merchant Service Guild and its Predecessors* (Wellington, The Guild, 1990).

Gavin McLean, *The Southern Octopus: The Rise of a Shipping Empire* (Wellington, New Zealand Ship and Marine Society and Wellington Harbour Board Maritime Museum, 1990).

Ministry of Foreign Affairs and Trade, *South Pacific Trade and Economic Prospects* (Wellington, MFAT, 1994)

Barry Pemberton, *Australian Coastal Shipping* (Melbourne, Melbourne University Press, 1979).

Periodicals

Business News, July 1980.
Dominion, Wellington, 11 May 1977.
Evening Post, Wellington, 11 May 1977.
Fiji Times, Suva, 15 September 1971, 2 May 1981.

Islands Business, October 1983.

National Business Review, Auckland, 23 July 1973, 24 November 1980, 8 December 1980, 21 February 1983, 23 April 1984.

New Zealand Herald, Auckland, 3 March 1978, 28 June 1984.

New Zealand Marine News, Wellington, 1979–present.

New Zealand Shipping Gazette, 1987–1998.

Pacific Islands Monthly, June 1975, October 1983.

Pacific Newsletter, 24 February 1979.

Post Courier (Papua New Guinea), 10 May 1984.

The Press, Christchurch, 16 September 1971.

Radio Australia, News Summary, 24 April 1984.

Radio New Zealand, Morning Report, Transcript of interview with Harry Julian, 2YA, 7.00 am, 2 March 1982.

Savali, 'PFL Disagreement to be Resolved at Tuvalu', 10 August 1984.

Tonga Chronicle, 16 September 1976.

Interviews

Ormond Eyre, long-time PFL manager, 3 March 1998.

Rod Gates, former New Zealand diplomat and High Commissioner to Fiji, 11 December 1997.

Francis Hong Tiy, former PFL employee, 3 March 1998.

Michael Hirschfeld, former PFL director, 5 November 1997.

Harry Julian, former PFL chairman and long-time shipowner, 12 December 1997.

His Excellency Ratu Sir Kamisese Mara, 2 March 1998.

Dave Morgan, President of the New Zealand Seafarers' Union, 13 October 1997.

Taniela Tufui, Secretary to Government of Tonga and Chairman PFL 1985–1998, 11 August 1997 and 6 March 1998.

Illustrations Acknowledgements

All illustrations courtesy Pacific Forum Line unless listed below.

Alexander Turnbull Library (ATL 996), 8 (ATL F18861 $\frac{1}{4}$), 9 (ATL 996) xvi
Colin Amodeo 15
Crown Copyright 2
Gordon Dewsnap 40, 41
Evening Post, **Wellington** 14, and **Mrs Pat Lodge** 66
Fiji Times 59
Hamburg Süd 34
Islands Business 67.
Nigel Kirby 10, 43, 57, 84, 86, 103 (bottom), 107
Nigel Kirby Collection 89
John MacLennan 110 (both photographs)
Ministry of Foreign Affairs, Wellington xviii
Ministry of Information, Suva xvi
National Archives, Wellington 8, 9
New Zealand Listener 55
New Zealand Shipping Gazette 78, 79, 80, 81, 82
PNG Post Courier 29
South Pacific Forum Secretariat 6, 21, 23, 24, 37, 65
Mahe Tupouniua 7

Appendix I

Pacific Forum Line Board of Directors

1977

T. H. Tufui (Tonga), R. P. Shea (New Zealand), J. H. Bowering (Papua New Guinea), Captain J. L. Harrison (Fiji), E. Tsitsi (Nauru), N. Slade* (Samoa).

1978

T. H. Tufui (Tonga), R. P. Shea (NZ), Captain P. King (PNG), Captain J. L. Harrison (Fiji), E. Tsitsi (Nauru), N. Slade* (Samoa), R. Chapman† (Cook Islands).

1979

T. H. Tufui (Tonga), R. P. Shea (NZ), Captain P. King (PNG), Captain J. L. Harrison (Fiji), Captain M. Bradshaw (Nauru), N. Slade* (Samoa), R. Chapman† (Cook Islands).

1980

T. H. Tufui* (Tonga), R. P. Shea (NZ), Captain P. King (PNG), N. Slade*/ H. Retzlaff (Samoa).

1981

T. H. Tufui/J. Riechelman (Tonga), H. L. Julian* (NZ), J. Gaius (PNG), H. Retzlaff (Samoa).

1982

T. H. Tufui (Tonga), H. L. Julian* (NZ), J. Gaius (PNG), H. Retzlaff (Samoa).

1983

T. H. Tufui (Tonga), H. L. Julian* (NZ), J. Gaius/G. Zurenouc (PNG), H. Retzlaff (Samoa).

1984

T. H. Tufui* (Tonga), H. L. Julian*/M. Hirschfeld (NZ), G. Zurenouc (PNG), T. Laumea (Samoa).

1985

T. H. Tufui* (Tonga), M. Hirschfeld (NZ), G. Zurenouc (PNG), T. Laumea (Samoa).

1986

T. H. Tufui* (Tonga), M. Hirschfeld (NZ), J. Gaius (PNG), H. Kiss (Fiji), O. Menke (Nauru), H. Retzlaff (Samoa), J. Caffery† (Cook Islands).

1987

T. H. Tufui* (Tonga), M. Hirschfeld (NZ), J. Gaius (PNG), H. Kiss (Fiji), H. Retzlaff (Samoa), Captain Murdoch† (Kiribati).

1988

T. H. Tufui* (Tonga), M. Hirschfeld (NZ), B. K. Amini (PNG), H. Kiss (Fiji), H. Retzlaff/T. F. Sapolu (Samoa), Captain Murdoch† (Kiribati).

1989

T. H. Tufui* (Tonga), M. Hirschfeld (NZ), B. K. Amini (PNG), H. Kiss (Fiji), T. F. Sapolu (Samoa), Captain Bowman† (Solomon Islands).

1990

T. H. Tufui* (Tonga), M. Hirschfeld (NZ), B. K. Amini (PNG), H. Kiss (Fiji), M. Moses (Nauru), T. F. Sapolu (Samoa), K. Kolone† (Tuvalu).

1991

T. H. Tufui* (Tonga), M. Hirschfeld (NZ), B. K. Amini (PNG), H. Kiss (Fiji), M. Moses (Nauru), T. F. Sapolu/M. R. Drake (Samoa), Hon. K. D. Lemari† (Marshall Islands).

1992

T. H. Tufui* (Tonga), M. Hirschfeld/P. T. Kiely (NZ), B. K. Amini (PNG), A. Vocea (Fiji), M. Moses (Nauru), M. R. Drake (Samoa), T. Kingi† (Niue).

1993

T. H. Tufui* (Tonga), P. T. Kiely (NZ), G. Zurenouc (PNG), A. Vocea/ M. Bainimarama (Fiji), M. Moses (Nauru), M. R. Drake (Samoa), H. Puna† (Cook Islands).

1994

T. H. Tufui* (Tonga), P. T. Kiely (NZ), G. Zurenouc (PNG), M. Bainimarama/ A. Vocea (Fiji), M. Moses (Nauru), M. R. Drake (Samoa), T. Tokataake† (Kiribati).

1995

T. H. Tufui* (Tonga), P. T. Kiely (NZ), G. Zurenouc (PNG), A. Vocea (Fiji), M. Moses (Nauru), M. R. Drake (Samoa), Hon. K. D. Lemari† (Marshall Islands).

1996

T. H. Tufui* (Tonga), P. T. Kiely (NZ), M. Tamarua (PNG), A. Vocea (Fiji), M. Moses (Nauru), M. R. Drake/P. Fepulea'i (Samoa), B. Punu† (Niue).

1997

T. H. Tufui* (Tonga), P. T. Kiely (NZ), M. Tamarua (PNG), A. Vocea (Fiji), Captain M. Bradshaw (Nauru), P. Fepulea'i (Samoa), P. Hauia† (Solomon Islands).

1998

T. H. Tufui* (Tonga), P. T. Kiely (NZ), M. Tamarua/C. Rupen (PNG), A. Vocea (Fiji), Captain M. Bradshaw (Nauru), P. Fepulea'i (Samoa), U. Sinapati† (Tuvalu).

*denotes chairman.
†denotes rotating member.

Appendix II

1998 Shareholding

Country	Number of Shares	Percentage Holding
Cook Islands	127,417	0.6
Fiji	4,803,859	23.0
Kiribati	733,165	3.5
Marshall Islands	772,500	3.7
New Zealand	4,840,500	23.1
Nauru	72,500	0.3
Niue	72,500	0.3
Papua New Guinea	6,047,524	28.9
Samoa	1,552,826	7.4
Solomon Islands	126,430	0.6
Kingdom of Tonga	1,271,956	6.1
Tuvalu	488,405	2.3
Total	20,909,582	

Appendix III

Dates and Venues of South Pacific Forum Meetings

1971	Wellington, New Zealand
1972	Canberra, Australia
1972	Suva, Fiji
1973	Apia, Samoa
1974	Rarotonga, Cook Islands
1975	Nuku'alofa, Tonga
1976	Aiwo, Nauru
1977	Port Moresby, Papua New Guinea
1978	Alofi, Niue
1979	Honiara, Solomon Islands
1980	Tarawa, Kiribati
1981	Port Vila, Vanuatu
1982	Rotorua, New Zealand
1983	Canberra, Australia
1984	Funafuti, Tuvalu
1985	Rarotonga, Cook Islands
1986	Suva, Fiji
1987	Apia, Samoa
1988	Nuku'alofa, Tonga
1989	Tarawa, Kiribati
1990	Port Vila, Vanuatu
1991	Pohnpei, Federated States of Micronesia
1992	Honiara, Solomon Islands
1993	Nauru
1994	Brisbane, Australia
1995	Madang, Papua New Guinea
1996	Majuro, Marshall Islands
1997	Rarotonga, Cook Islands
1998	Pohnpei, Federated States of Micronesia

Appendix IV

Vessels

Builder/Place-Yard number. Date of launch-completion. grt/nrt/dwt* Initial names/owners/(managers) including PFL involvement	Dates with PFL	Subsequent names/owners/(managers) after PFL involvement
TAULOTO II G. Dimitrov Shipyard. Varna-206. –1970. 43667/2582/4951. Ex *Safia*: Papuan Liner Services Pty Ltd (Karlander (Australia) Pty Ltd), Port Moresby (1970–73). *Tauloto II*: same owner/manager, Nuku'alofa (1973–79).	4/5/78–8/6/79	*Koheng*: Alioth Shipping Co SA (Grit Enterprises Ltd), Panama (1979–83). Same owner (Taheng Sg Co Ltd), Panama (1983–88), Kingstown (1988–90). *Xinheng*: Xinheng Sg Co Ltd (Worlder Sg Ltd), Kingstown (1990–92). *Sunjoy*: J. R. Shipping SA, Panama (1992–).
TOA MOANA At. et Ch. Du Havre. Havre-192. 7/1968–12/1968 1191/640/1771. Ex *Jogela*: I/S Lars Rej Johansen & Knut. A. Knutsen (Lars Rej Johansen), Oslo (1968–69). ms *Jogela* Tunnecke Schiffs (N. F. Cordes & Co), Bremen (1969–74). *Toa Moana*: Shipping Corporation of NZ Ltd, Wellington (1974–81).	15/5/78–27/12/79	*Temehani II*: Société Anonyme de Navigation Temehani, Papeete (1981–).
MATAORA Wiestern Schps. Unie NV Hellevoetsluis-66. 1/1957–4/1957 297/131/366. Ex *Fiducia II*: Firma C. Minnaar (Ripmeester & Co NV), Rotterdam (1957–1969). *Fiducia*: T. Boersma (Ripmeester & Co NV), Groningen (1969–70). R/A Uman (N. K. Mattson), Halbevik (1970–77). *Mataora*: Silk & Boyd Ltd, Suva (1977–78), Nuku'alofa (1978–).	78–78	
WOOLGAR Varna Shipyard 'Georgi Dimitrov' Varna-208. 6/1970–10/1970 2755/1284/4948. Built for Borges Rederi A/S Tonsberg (1970–82).	8/7/78–20/4/79	(Chartered by Nauru in place of *Eigamoya*). *Woolga*: Samta Pte Ltd, Singapore (1982–83). *Yang Zi Jiang 4*: China Yangtze River Sg Co, Wuhan (1983–).
OKEANIS Eleusis Shipyards S.A. Eleusis-1.0.003. 6/1972–4/1973 3717/2162/5840. Built for International Merchant Corp (Andreadis (UK) Ltd), Chios (1973–79). Trading & General Investment Corp (Andreadis (UK) Ltd), Chios (1979–87).	28/5/79–1/2/80	(Replaced *Woolgar*). *Blue Ocean I*: Blue Ocean Lines Ltd, Chittagong (1987–89). *Blue Ocean*: Same owner, Chittagong (1989–96). *Ocean I*: Fair Shipping lines Pte Ltd, Chittagong (1996–98). Silverstar Marine Ltd (Murmansk Shipping Co), Kingstown (1998–).

*grt= gross registered tonnage; nrt=net registered tonnage; dwt=deadweight.

131

MORESBY CHIEF
Husumer Schiffs. Husum-1406.
7/1972–9/1972   1634/1082/2906.
Ex: *Lindinger Brilliant*: Rederiet Lindinger A/S,
Copenhagen (1972–78).
Petra: Jordan Maritime Navigation Co Ltd, Aqaba
(1978–79).
Moresby Chief: Mainport Cargoes Pty Ltd (Papua
New Guinea Shipping Corp Pty Ltd), Port
Moresby (1979–81). Papua New Guinea Shipping
Corp Pty Ltd, Port Moresby (1979–89).

| 6/79–7/79 21/5/80–26/6/80 | (one voyage 1979 due to late arrival of *Forum Niugini* and one voyage 1980 to uplift produce). *Mahasen*: P.T. Pelayaran Naga Bangka, Colombo (1989–). (Laid up, surveys overdue 1/1995.) |

FORUM NIUGINI
J. J. Sietas Schiffs, Hamburg-623.
9/1969–10/1969   3894/2541/4230.
Ex: *Arosia*: Partenreederei MS *Arosia*. (Peter
Dohle), Hamburg (1969–79).
(11/8/73–18/9/73 at Hamburg being
lengthened).
Forum Niugini: Concordia Shipping Pty Ltd
(Papua New Guinea Sg Corp Pty Ltd), Port
Moresby (1979–80).

| 7/8/79–20/4/80 | *Niugini Chief*: Concordia Shipping Pty Ltd (Papua New Guinea Shipping Corp Pty Ltd), Port Moresby (1980–81). *Dexena*: Dexterson Shipping Co Ltd, Limassol (1981–87). *Brasiliana*: Weston Maritime Ltd (Multifleet Marine Ltd), Nassau (1987–87). *Zim Brasiliana*: Same owner, Nassau (1987–88). *Brasiliana*: Same owner, Nassau (1988–91). *Swee Long Satu*: Sim Swee Joo Shipping Sendirian Berhad, Labuan (1991–). |

FORUM SAMOA
J. J. Sietas Schiffs, Hamburg-893.
7/1979–10/1979   3838/1748/5536.
Built for Government of The Independent State of
Samoa (Samoa Shipping Services Ltd), Apia
(1979–)

| 17/10/79– | To ownership of Torbjorn Benestad, Panama, (1998–). (Remains under charter to PFL.) |

FUA KAVENGA
J. J. Sietas Schiffs, Hamburg-894.
10/1979–12/1979   3841/1751/5536.
Built for South Pacific Forum Lines (Columbus
Overseas Service Pty Ltd), Nuku'alofa (1979–81).
The Shipping Corp of Polynesia Ltd, Nuku'alofa
(1981–84). Government of the Kingdom of Tonga
(Shipping Corp of Polynesia), Nuku'alofa
(1984–86). Same owner (Columbus Overseas
Service Pty Ltd) Nuku'alofa (1986–88). The Ship-
ping Corp of Polynesia Ltd (Columbus Overseas
Service Pty Ltd), Nuku'alofa (1988–).

| 4/12/79– | Replaced *Okeanis*. |

FORUM NEW ZEALAND
Kagoshima Dock & I. W. Co, Kagoshima-122.
8/1978–12/1978   6226/3875/6945.
Ex: *Strider Isis*: Strider 9 Ltd (Sea Containers
Chartering Ltd), Hamilton, Bermuda (1978–87).
Forum New Zealand: Same owner, Hamilton,
Bermuda (1980–87).

| 23/3/80–3/87 | (Replaced *Toa Moana*, chartered/managed by The Shipping Corp of NZ Ltd). *Strider Isis*: Strider 9 Ltd (Sea Management Services—SMS), Hamilton, Bermuda (1987–90). K/S SC Strider Isis (V Ships (UK) Ltd), Nassau (1990–96). *Pelranger*: Pelranger Maritime Inc (Sarlis Container Services SA), Piraeus (1996–). |

BENJAMIN BOWRING
Aalborg Vaerft A/S, Aalborg-96.
1/1952–5/1952   1184/550/1285.
Ex: *Kista Dan*: J. Lauritzen, Esbjerg (1952–56).
Martin Karlsen: Martin Karlsen A/S, Alesund
(1966–68), Karlsen Shipping Co Ltd, Halifax
(1968–79).
Benjamin Bowring: Bowring SS Co Ltd (Transglobe Expedition Ltd), London (1979–82).

4/5/80–15/11/80   (Chartered for the inter-island service from Suva.)
To ownership of the Bearcreek Oil & Shipping Co
(Transglobe Expedition Ltd), London (1982–83).
Arctic Gael: Freighters & Tankers Ltd (Halba
Shipping Ltd), Hamilton, Bermuda (1983–84).
Olympiakos: Same owner, Hamilton, Bermuda
(1984–85). Marnato Cia Nav SA (Goulandris
Agencies), Panama (1985–).
(Removed from Shipping Registers 1989—con-
verted to a yacht. By 12/1997 reported registered
in London, purchased by a British businessman
and presented to a former director of Greenpeace
for use in the removal of rubbish from
Antarctica.)

AI SOKULA
D. & J. Boot Schps, Alphen-1267.
8/1961–9/1961   400/204/600.
Ex: *Boezemsingel*: Scheepsexpl, Onderneming
'Boezemsingel' (Invoer-en-Transportonderneming
'Invotra' NV), Rotterdam (1961–62). P. A. van Es
& Co NV, Rotterdam (1962–66).
Ai Sokula: Island Industries Ltd, Suva (1966–70).
Island Transport Ltd, Suva (1970–77), Rabi Hold-
ings Ltd, Suva (1977–81).

30/1/81–26/2/81   Ran aground at 1955 hours, 22/2/1981 on Fafaofo
Atoll, Tokelaus. Driven further ashore by a
cyclone on 1/3/1981. Discharged and abandoned
high dry. (At the time of her loss, chartered by
Rabi Holdings to Wong's Shipping Company,
Suva, sub-chartered to the New Zealand Government (Foreign Affairs), and managed by PFL.)

NIVANGA
Hongkong and Whampoa Dock Co,
                              Hongkong-1010.
9/1961–1/1962   353/163/–.
Built for the Government of The Gilbert & Ellice
Islands Colony, Tarawa (1962–74), Government
of Tuvalu (Ministry of Home Affairs), Funafuti
(1974–89), Consort Shipping Line Ltd, Suva
(1989–90).

/81–10/88   (Tuvalu feeder service.)
Nivanga I: J. F. K. Holding Ltd, Suva (1990–94).
Neil Carter and Irene June Wright, Auckland
(1994–97). Detained at Auckland by the Maritime
Safety Authority 6/9/96. Advertised for sale
20/9/97 and sold to B. & B. Demolition Ltd who
broke her up at Marsden Wharf, Auckland,
11–12/1997.

TABU SORO
VEB Rosslauer Schiffs, Rosslau-3271.
          –11/1969   199/118/398.
Ex: *Heia*: Rederi A/S Osloagenturer (Lars Rej
Johansen), Oslo (1969–74).
Tabusoro: Government of Fiji (Marine Depart-
ment), Suva (1974–).

11/82–11/82   (Voyage charted from Fiji–East.)

MOANA RAOI
J. J. Sietas Schiffs, Hamburg-422.
2/1958–7/1958   561/392/970.
Launched as *Actuaria*: Pertenreederi Actuaria,
Hamburg.
Completed as *Ingrid Horn*: Horn & Co (Henrich
C. Horn), Hamburg (1958–65). Same owner
(Hamburg Sudamerikanische Dampfs), Hamburg
(1965–67). *Moanaraoi*: The Wholesale Society of
Betio, Tarawa, Gilbert & Ellice Islands, Suva
(1967–81). The Shipping Corporation of Kiribati,
Betio (1981–84), Suva (1984–87), Betio (1987–92).
Kiribati Shipping Services Ltd—KSSL, Betio
(1992–).

/83–10/88   (Voyage chartered only for Kiribati feeder
service.)

NEI MATABURO
Yokohama Yacht Co Ltd, Yokohama-824.
5/1984–7/1984   524/157/307.
Built for the Government of the Republic of
Kiribati (Ministry of Communications & Works),
Tarawa, (1984–88). The Shipping Corporation of
Kiribati, Betio, (1988–92). Kiribati Shipping Serv-
ices Ltd—KSSL, Betio, (1992–).

FORUM NEW ZEALAND II
Howaldtswerke-Deutsches Werft, Hamburg-97.
9/1976–1/1977   10991/7135/13880.
Laid down as: *Brabant*: Ernst Willner Container
GmbH & Cosima Reederei KGMS 'Brabant' (Pos-
eidon Schiffarhrts GmbH), Hamburg.
Renamed *Urundi* whilst fitting-out—same owner,
Hamburg.
Gulf Ranger: Same owner, Hamburg (1977–78).
Urundi: Same owner (DAL Deutsche Afrika-
Linien GmbH), Hamburg (1978–81).
Lanka Athula: Coronado Container Schiffahrts
GmbH & Co, Reederei KG M/S 'Brabant' (C. F.
Ahrenkiel), Hamburg (1981–83).
Lanka Amitha: Same owner, Hamburg
(1983–85).
Brabant: Same owner, Hamburg (1985–86).
Forum New Zealand II: The Shipping Corp. of NZ
Ltd (New Zealand Line), Wellington (1986–89).

NIVAGA II
Richards (Shipbuilders) Ltd, Lowestoft-576.
3/1988–7/1988   1043/314/590.
Built for the Government of Tuvalu (Ministry of
Home Affairs), Funafuti (1988–).

WEKA
Refer *Forum New Zealand II*

FORUM MICRONESIA
Carl B. Hoffmanns Mask, Esbjeg-55.
–/1984–1/1985   2151/645/1650.
Ex: *Svendborg Gold*: P/R Gold (Svendborg Enter-
prises ApS), Svendborg (1985–86).
Pumori: Riis Shipping ApS, Svendborg
(1986–86).
Svendborg Gold: P/R Gold (Svendborg Enterprises
ApS), Svendborg (1986–89).
Forum Micronesia: Same owner, Svendborg
(1989–93).

10/88–5/93

(Replaced *Moana Raoi* on Kiribati feeder
service.)

Chartered
26/1/87–9/3/89
Owned
9/3/89–6/8/93

(Replaced *Forum New Zealand*.)
Weka: Eckington Ltd (Denholm Ship Management
Ltd), Hongkong (1989–89).
Forum New Zealand II: Pacific Forum Line Ltd,
Hongkong (1989–93).
Anro Adelaide: Torsen Company Ltd (Anglo
Eastern Ship Management Ltd), Hongkong
1993–94).
MCC Conveyor: Same owner, Hongkong
(1994/95).
Khyber: Same owner, Hongkong (1995–97).
Maersk Arusha: Same owner, Hongkong
(1997–97).
X-Press Khyber: Same owner, Hongkong
(1997–).

10/88–5/93

(Replaced *Nivanga* on Tuvalu feeder service.)

14/1/89–6/89

24/1/89–4/93

Svendborg Gold: P/R Gold (Svendborg Enterprises
A/S), Svendborg (1993–).

STAR SIRANGER
Refer *Forum Papua New Guinea*.

7/90–9/90

FORUM PAPUA NEW GUINEA
Hyundai SB & Heavy Engineering Industrues
                                        Ulsan-1658.
6/1977–1/1978   12804/5401/17190.
Ex: *Antares*: Finska Angfartygs A/B, Helsingfors
(1978–79).
Chase One: Same owner, Helsingfors
(1979–79).
Antares: Same owner, Helsingfors (1979–87).
Star Sirius: Same owner, Helsingfors (1987–88).
Antares: Same owner, Helsingfors (1988–89).
Star Sirius: Westfal Larsen & Co A/S, Manila
(1989–89), Monrovia (1989–90).
Star Siranger: Royal Bonnett Investments Inc
(Westfal Larsen & Co A/S), Monrovia (1990–90).
Eckington Ltd (Pacific Forum Line (NZ) Ltd),
Hongkong (1990–90).
Forum Papua New Guinea: Eckington Ltd (Pacific
Forum Line (NZ) Ltd), Hongkong (1990–95).

9/90–5/95   *Clipper Golden Hind*: Ivy Nav Ltd (Kylco Maritime
                  Ltd), Monrovia (1995–).

THOR LISBETH
Svendborg Vaerft A/S, Svendborg-203.
1/1994–/1994   1395/547/2112.
Launched as *Lisbeth Riis*: Riis Shipping ApS,
Svendborg.
Completed as *Thor Lisbeth*: A/S Frederiksoen I
(Tonnevold & Clausen), Svendborg (1994–).

2/12/94–   (Joint charter arrangement with Cook Islands
                  National Line.)

SOCOFL STREAM
Kyokuyo Zosen KK, Chofu-376.
8/1992–10/1992   4885/2221/6311.
Built for Aurora Navigation SA (Unicom Management Services (Cyprus) Ltd), Panama (1992–94).
Same owner (Kamchatka Shipping Co). Petropavlovsk-Kamchatskiy (1994–95). Kamchatka
Shipping Co Ltd, Petropavlovsk-Kamchatskiy
(1995–)

5/95–5/96   (Joint service with Sofrana.)

FORUM TOKELAU
Stocznia Wisla, Gdansk-B457/01.
–/1971–2/1972   809/371/1063.
Ex: *Hajnowka*: Polska Zegulga Morska, Szczecin
(1972–76). Polska Zegula Baltycka, Kolobrzeg
(1976–93). Triad Enterprises S-ka z.o.o., Kolobrzeg
(1993–94). Trade Enterprises, Kolobrzeg
(1994–97).
Forum Tokelau: Pacific Forum Line (NZ) Ltd,
Avatiu (1997–).

27/3/97–

This list has been prepared just prior to publication and is as accurate as possible in view of the limited time
available.

Index of Vessels

Bold entries denote photographs or illustrations.

Index

Bold entries denote photographs or illustrations.